T0128024

Seven Lessons on
ARCHITECTURAL MORPHOGENESIS

Peter Magyar

IN MEMORIAM OF MY PARENTS, MARGIT AND JOZSEF

Order this book online at www.trafford.com
or email orders@trafford.com

Most Trafford titles are also available at major online book retailers.

Printed in the United States of America.

ISBN: 978-1-4669-8389-2 (sc)
ISBN: 978-1-4669-8391-5 (hc)
ISBN: 978-1-4669-8390-8 (e)

Library of Congress Control Number: 2013904285

Trafford rev. 03/07/2013

 www.trafford.com

North America & international
toll-free: 1 888 232 4444 (USA & Canada)
phone: 250 383 6864 ✦ fax: 812 355 4082

CONTENTS

Drawings speak in
many tongues. Lines
form the text
of this book.

THE PEAK HONG KONG

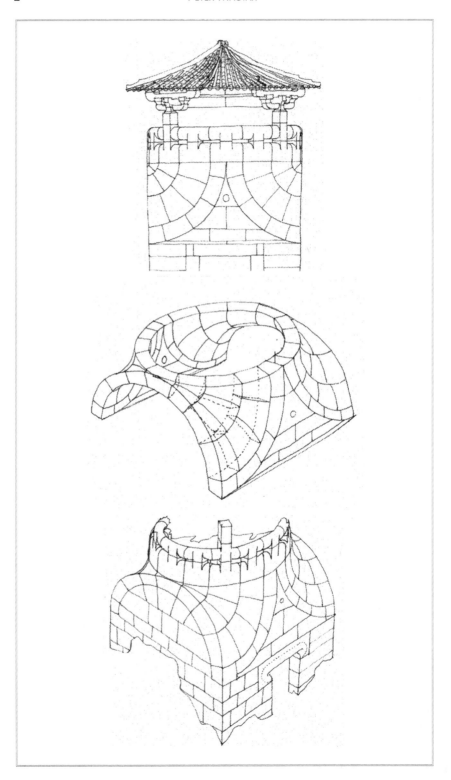

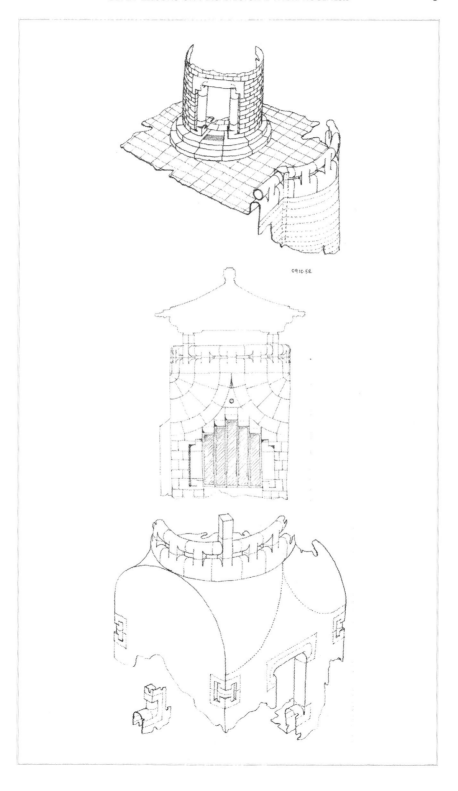

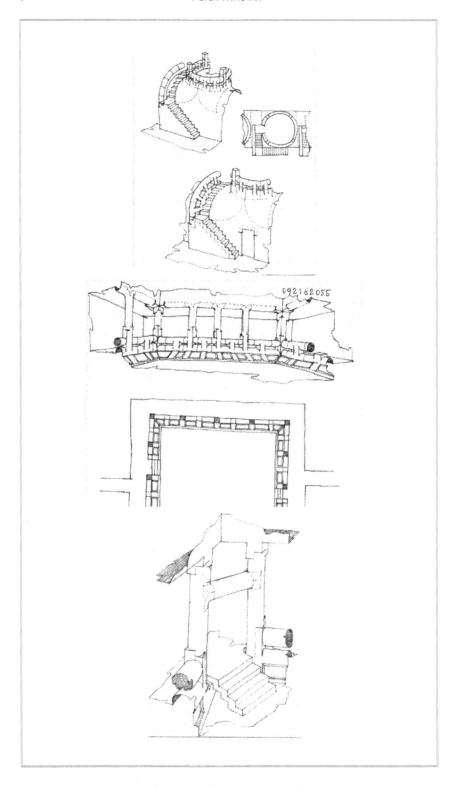

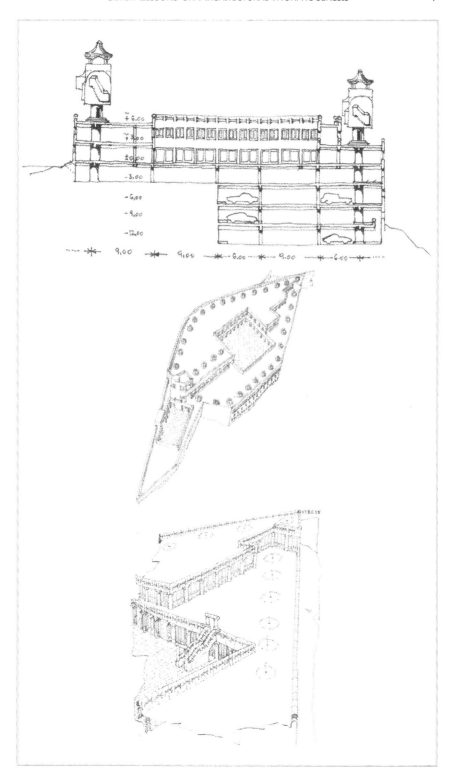

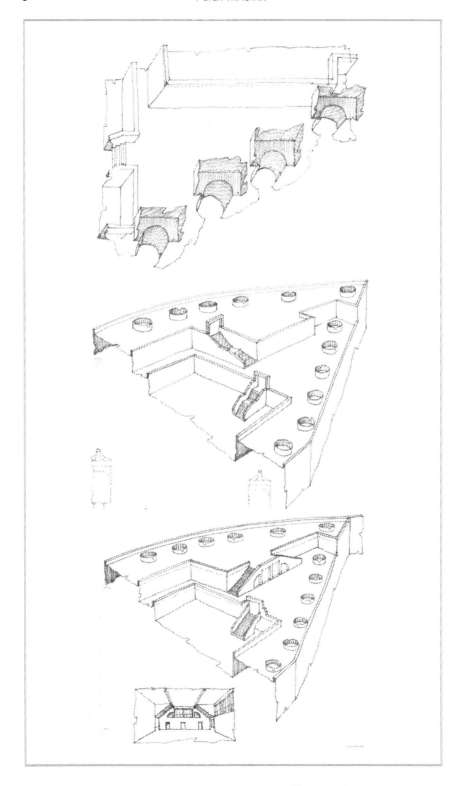

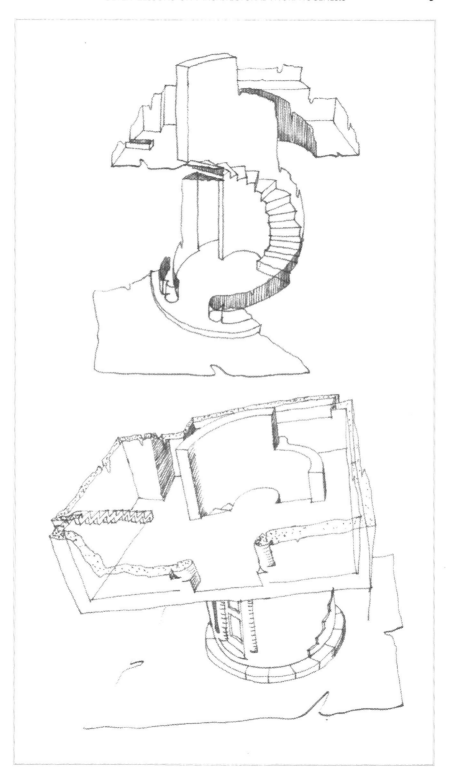

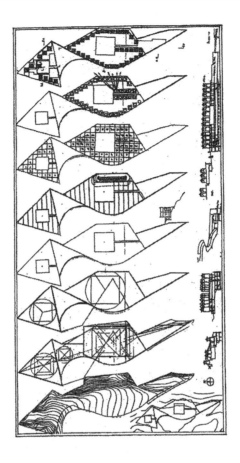

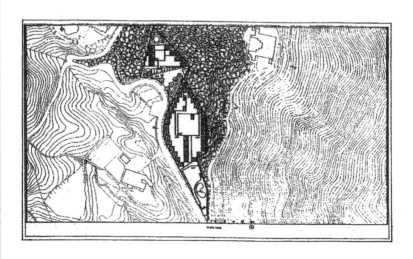

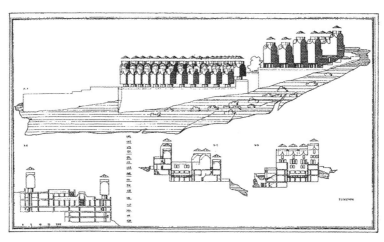

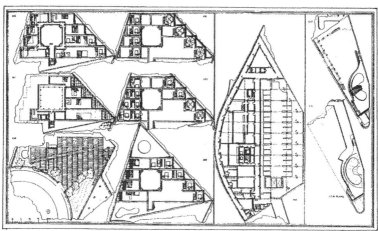

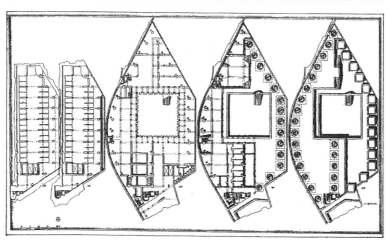

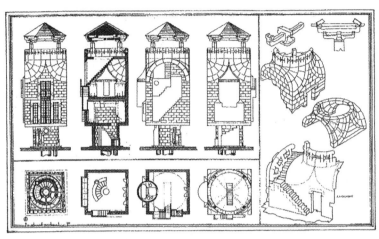

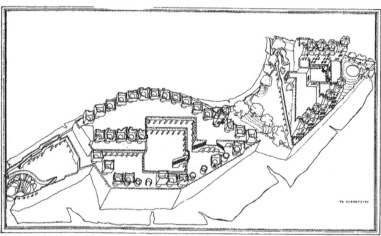

OPERA BASTILLE
PARIS

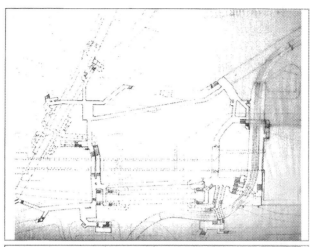

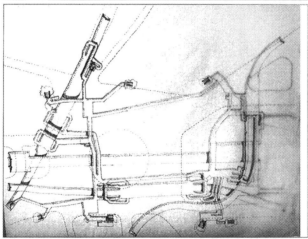

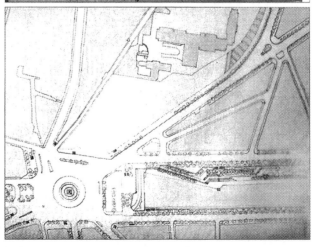

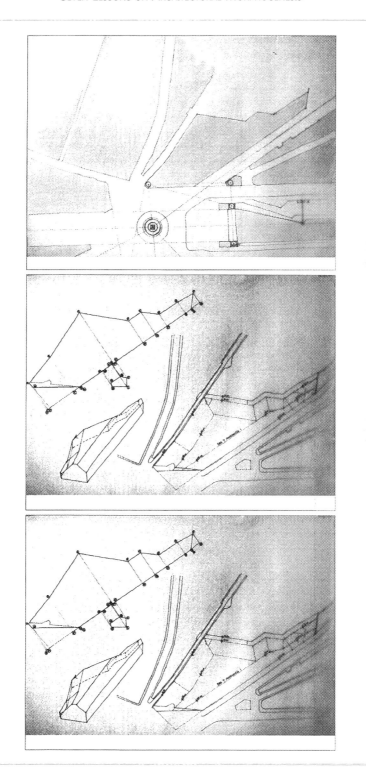

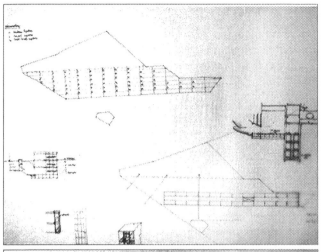

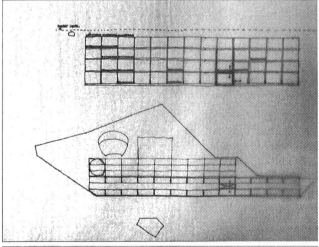

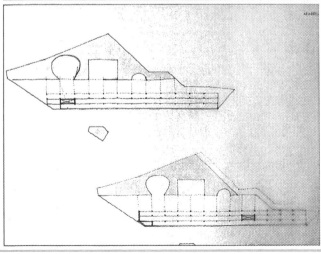

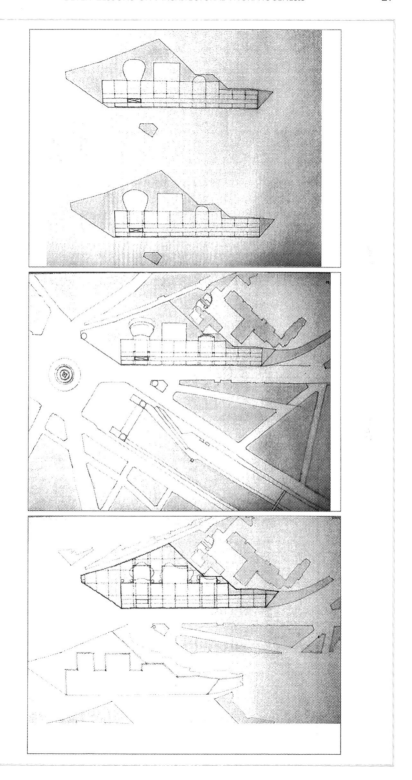

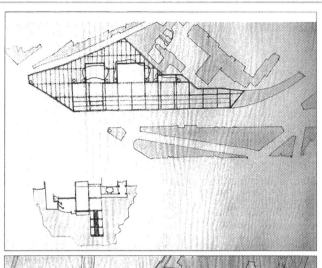

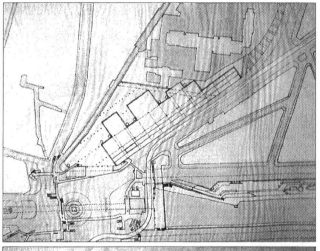

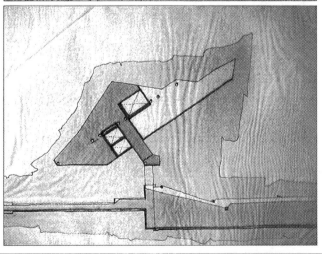

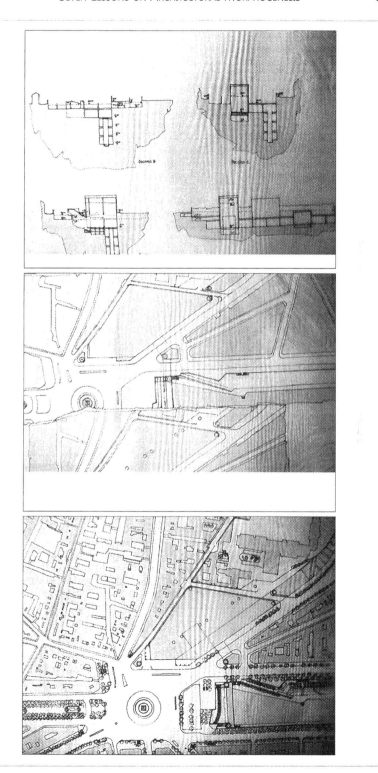

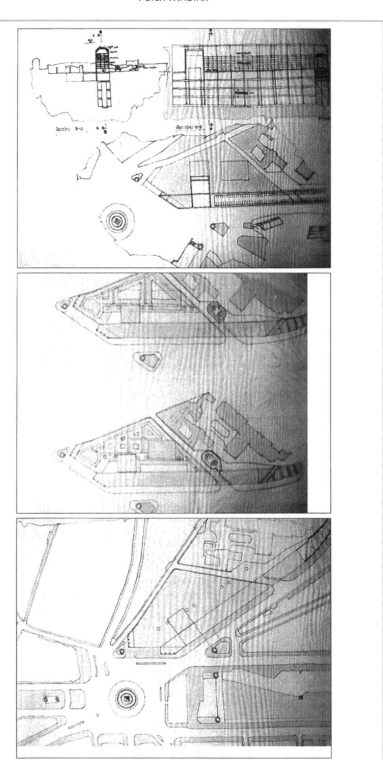

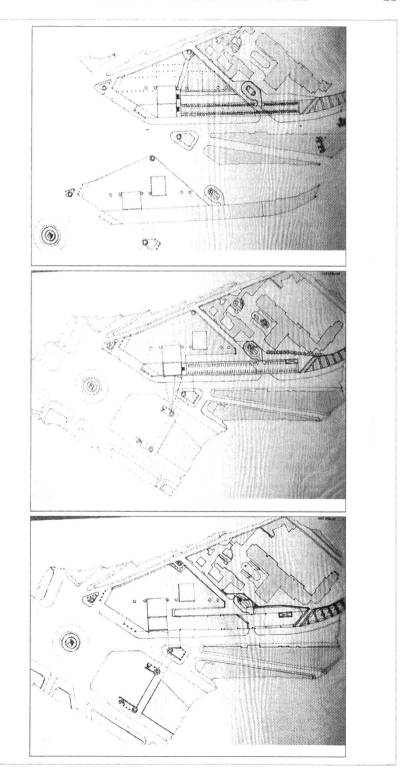

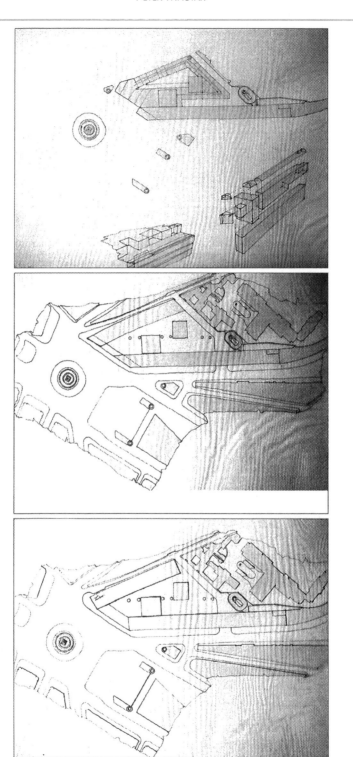

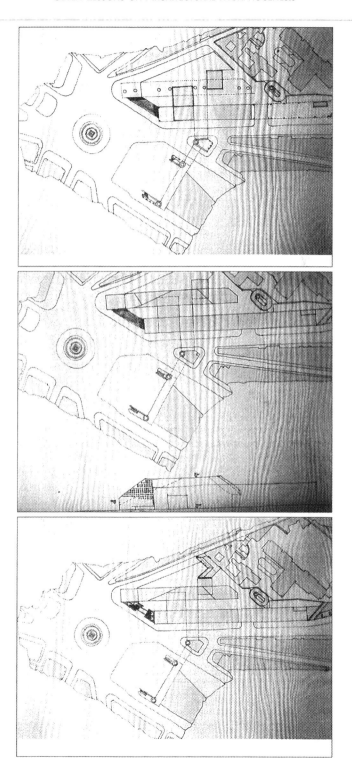

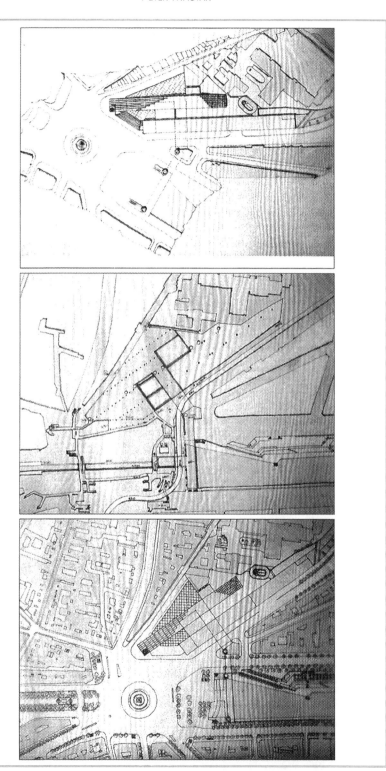

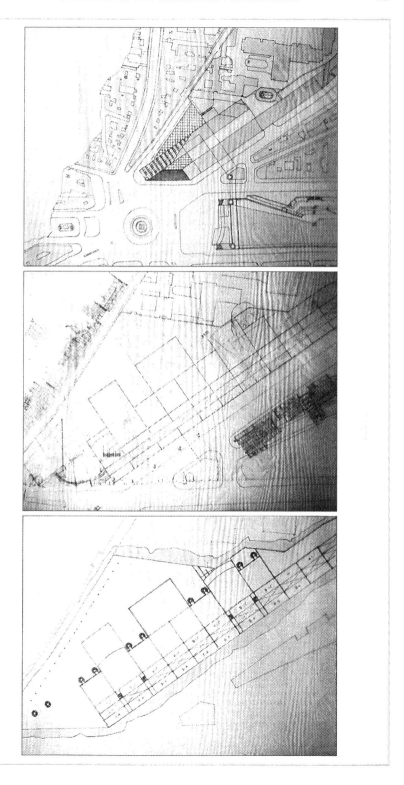

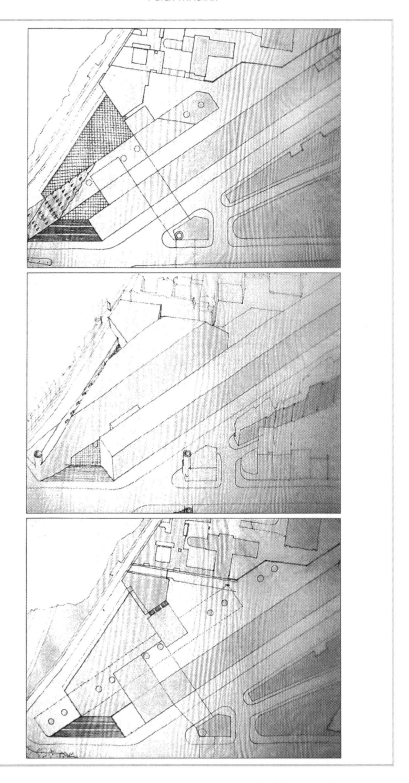

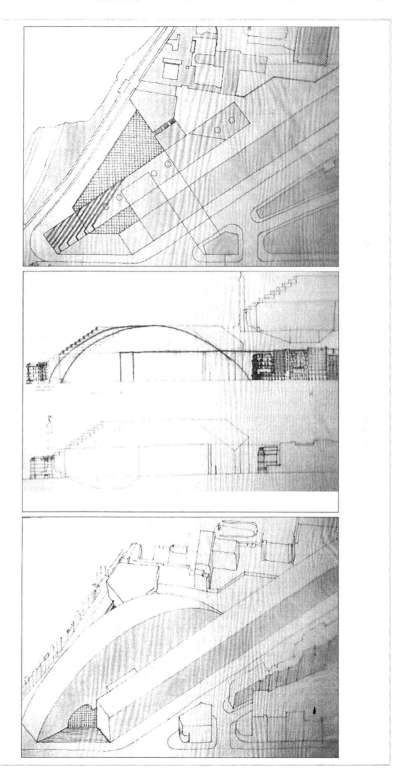

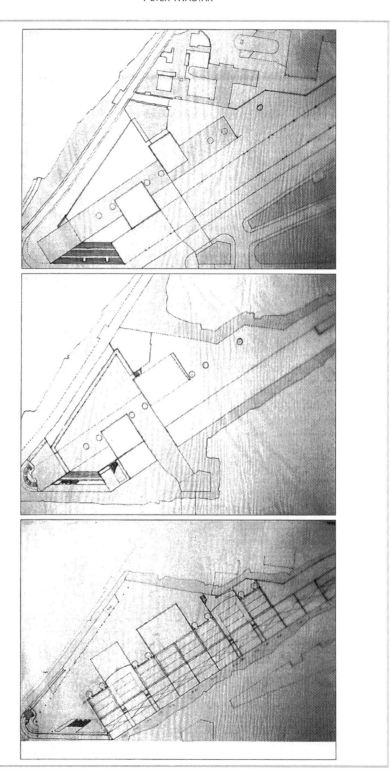

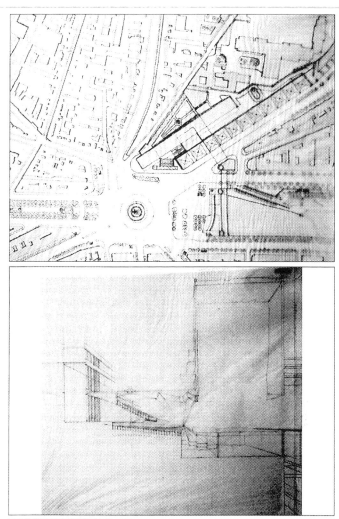

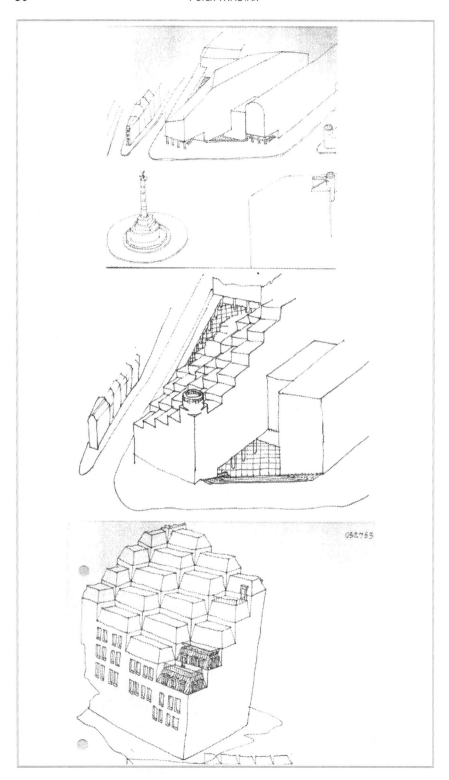

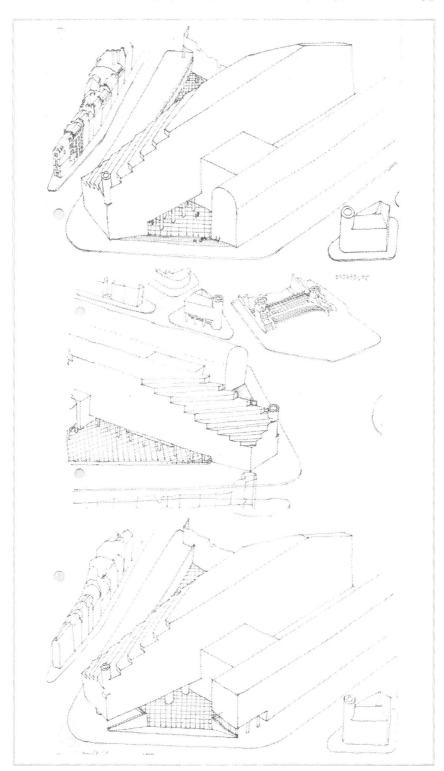

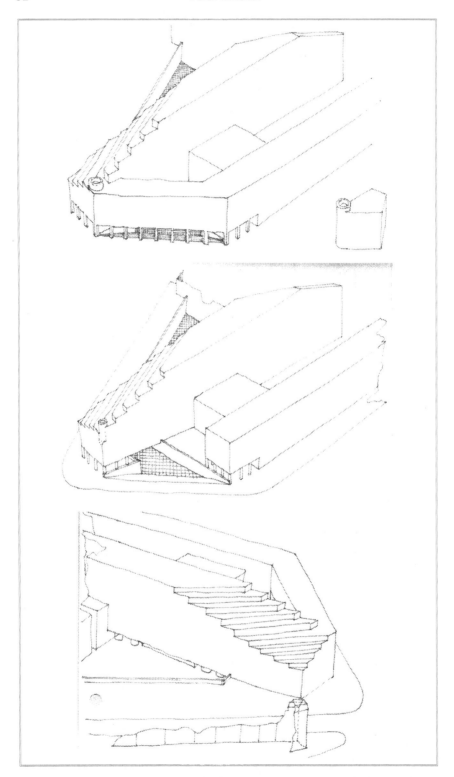

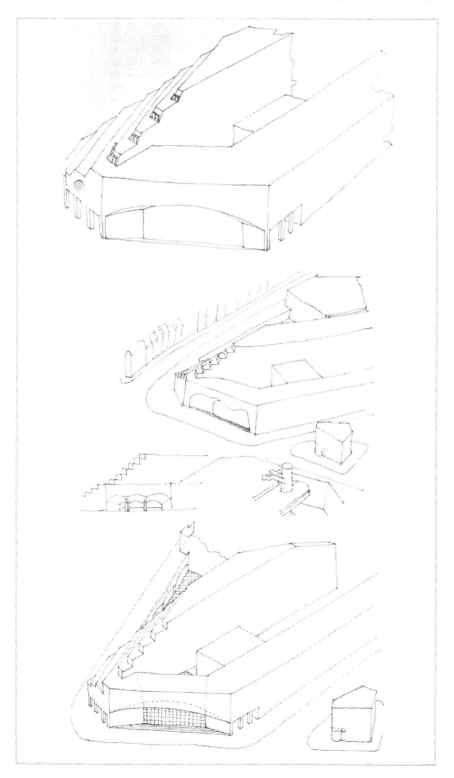

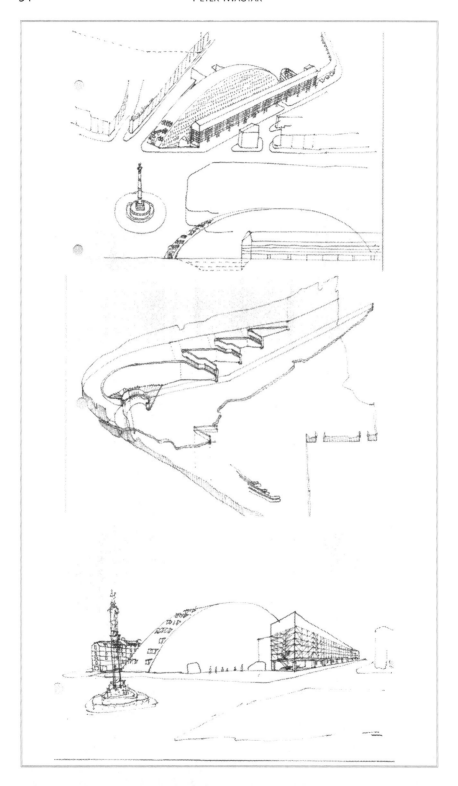

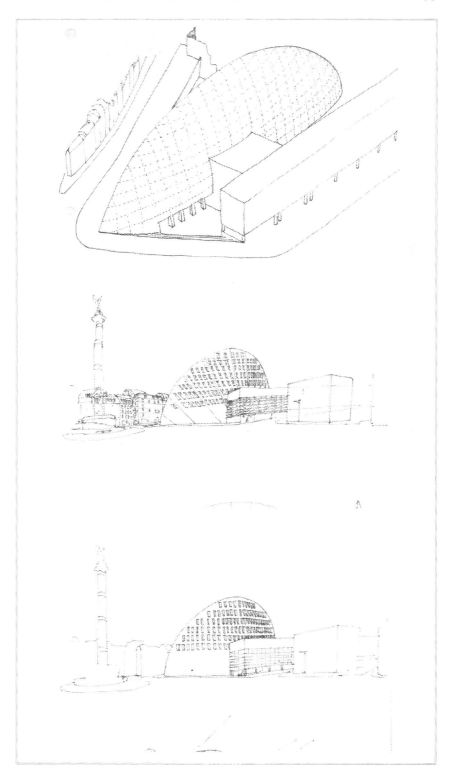

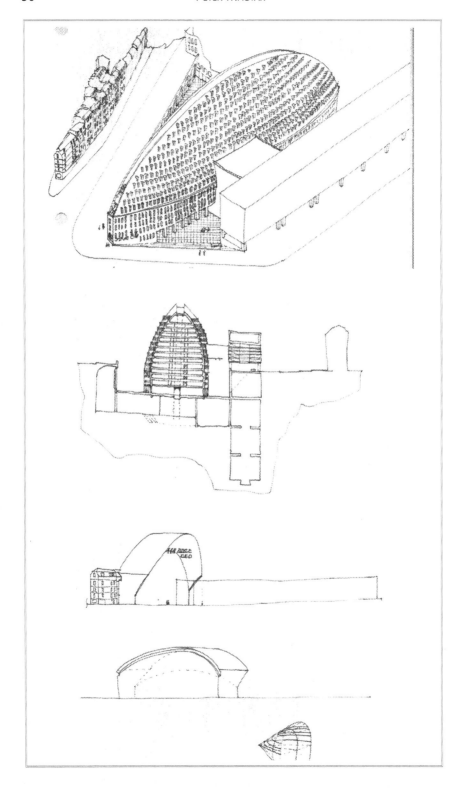

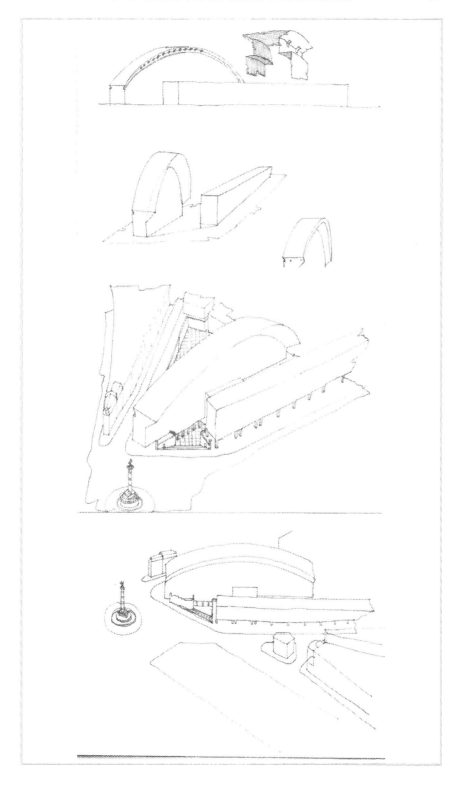

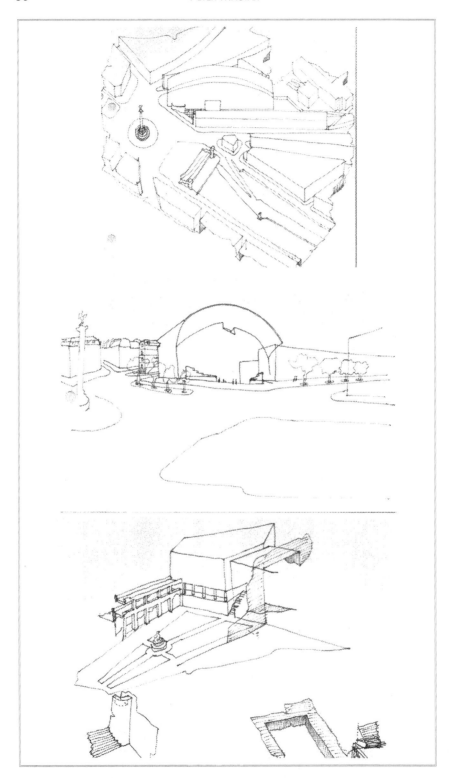

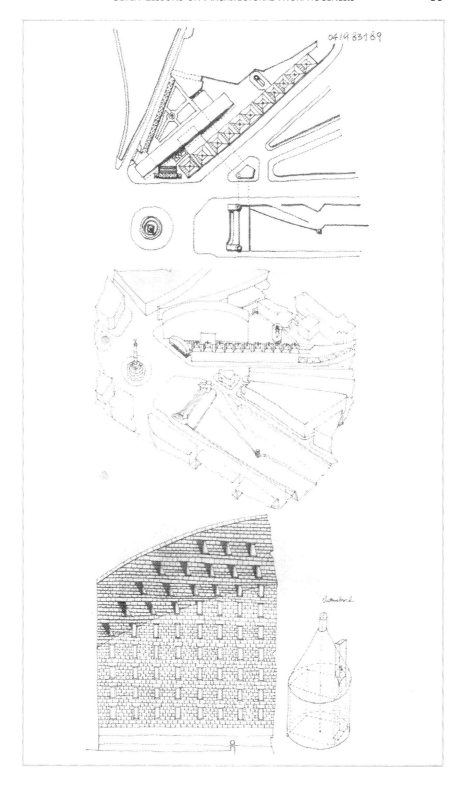

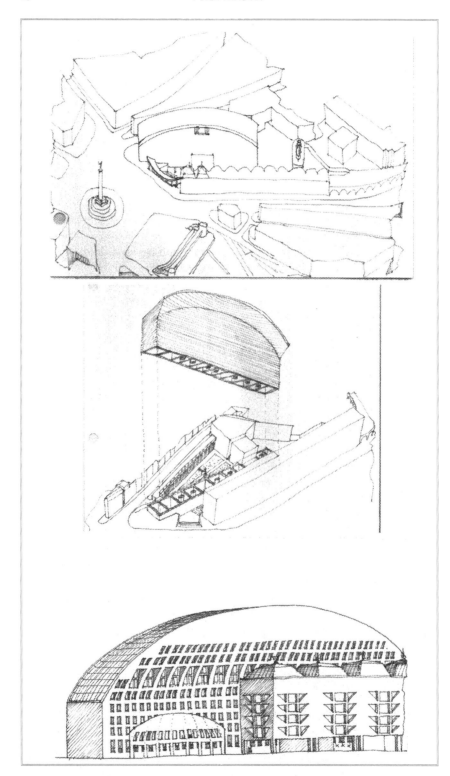

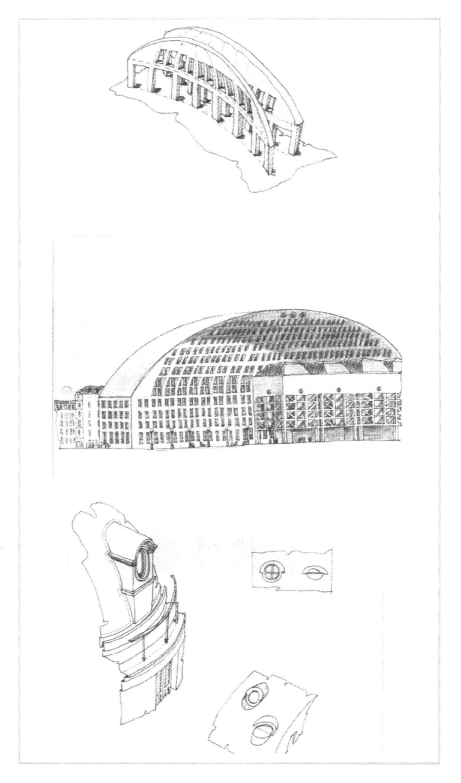

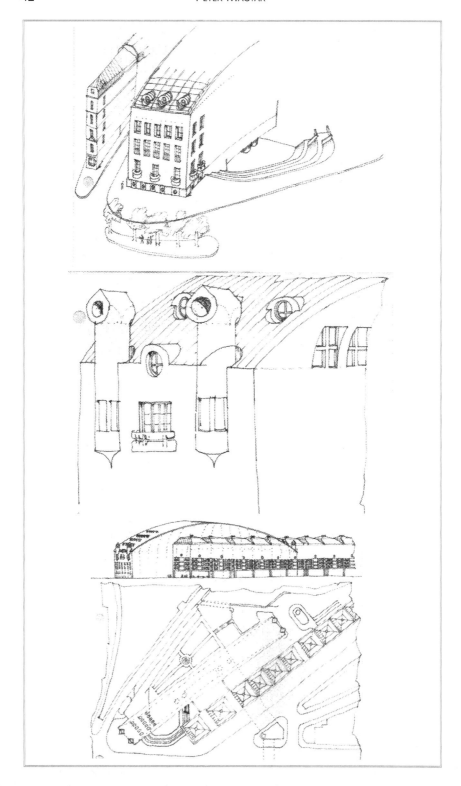

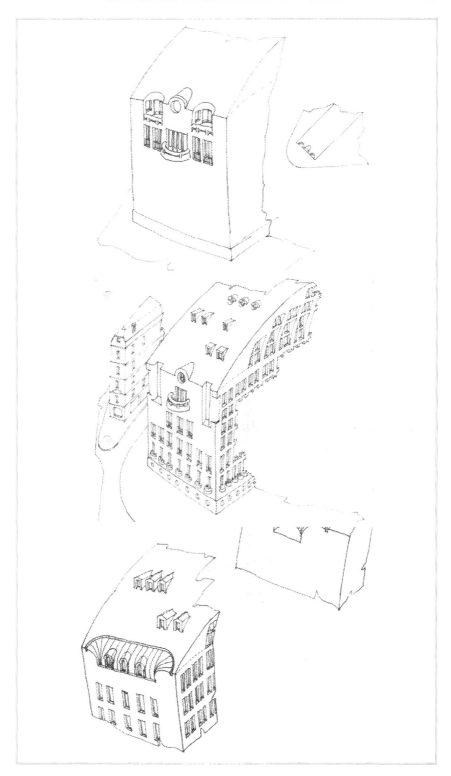

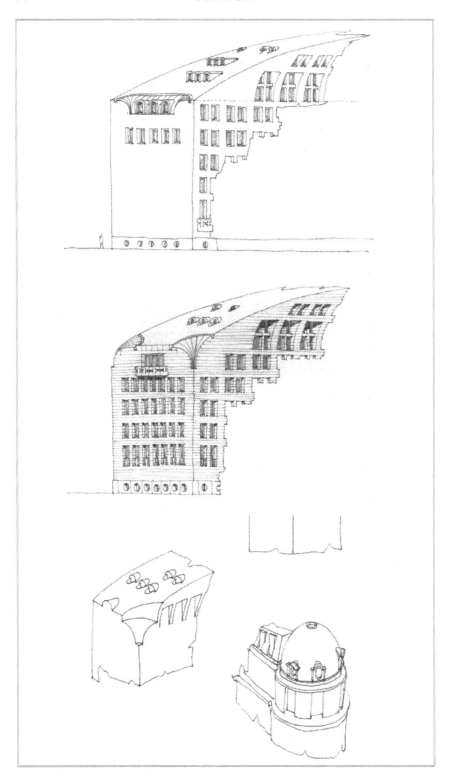

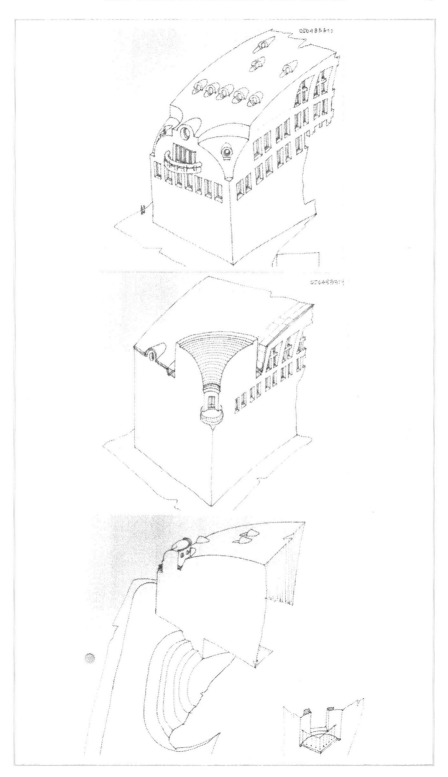

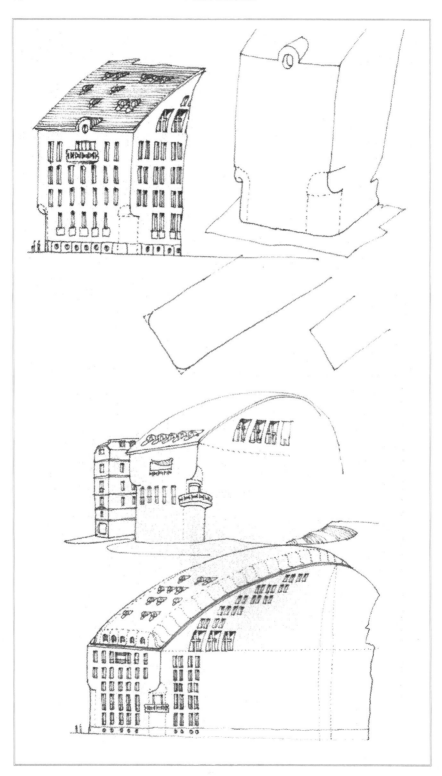

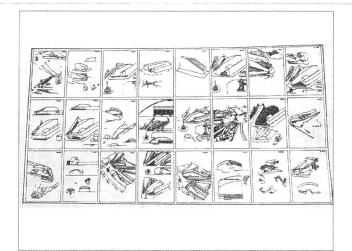

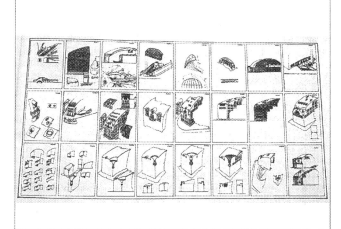

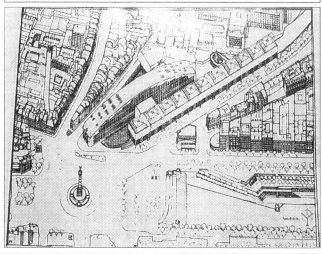

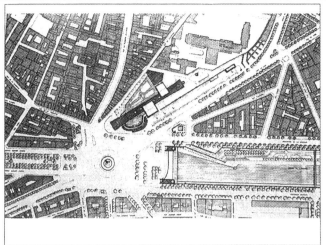

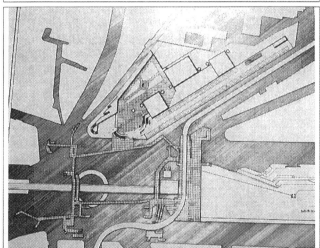

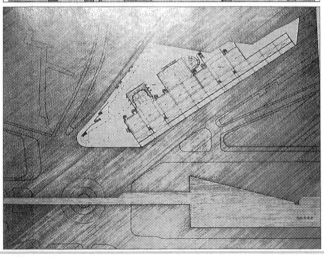

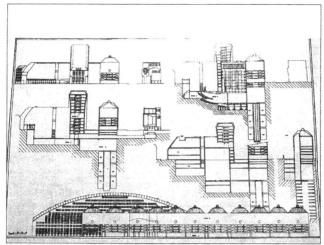

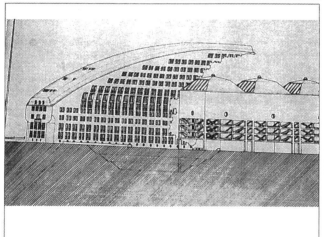

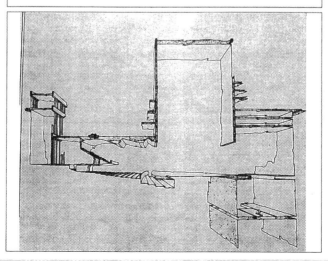

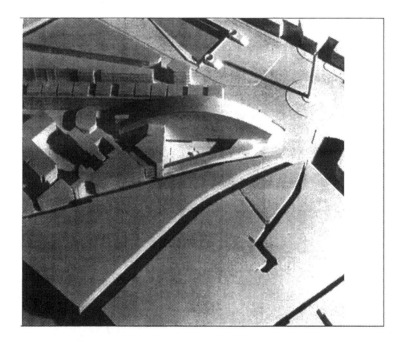

PUBLIC SAFETY BUILDING
PITTSBURGH, PA

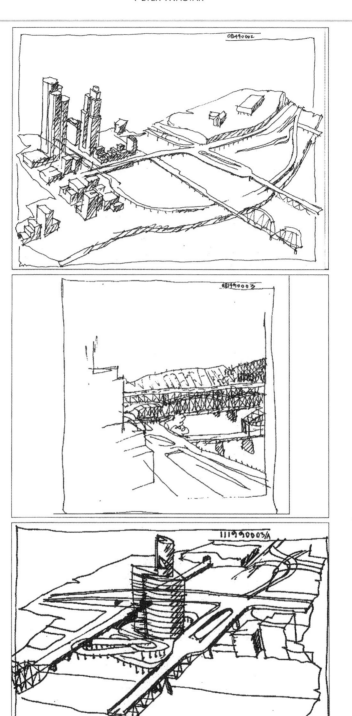

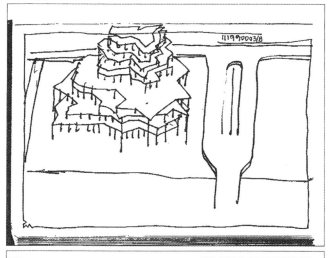

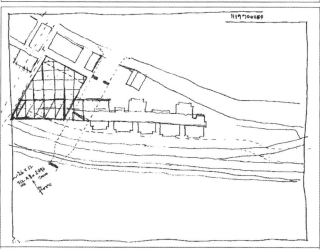

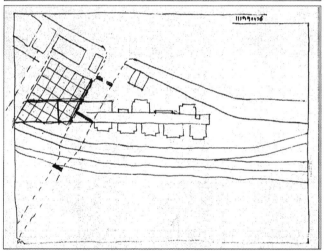

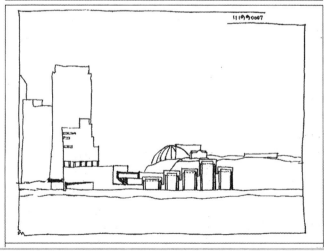

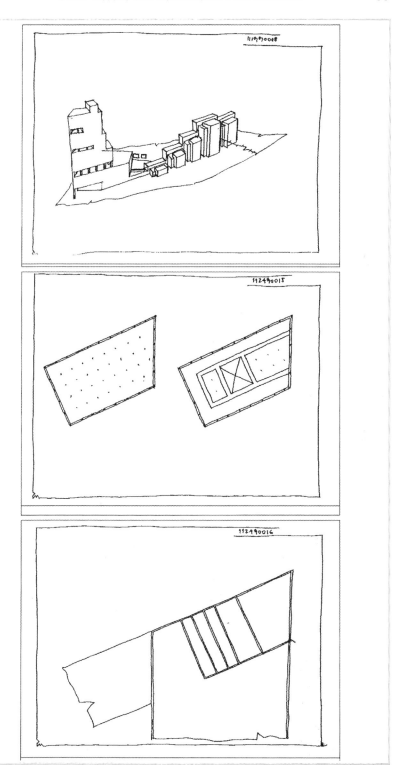

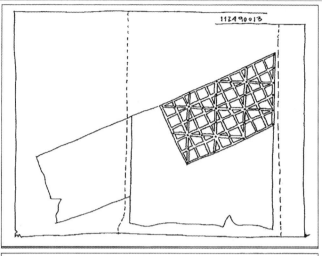

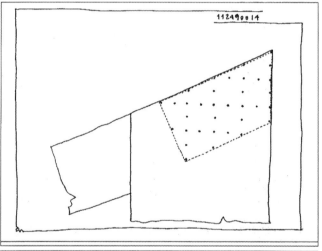

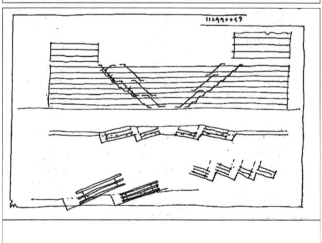

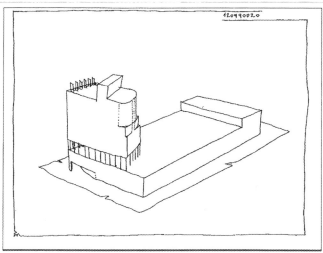

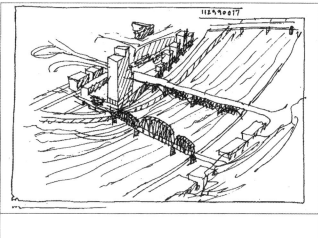

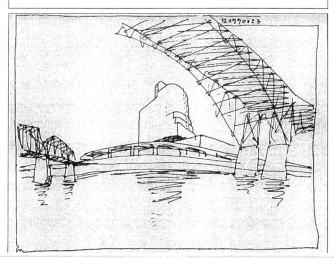

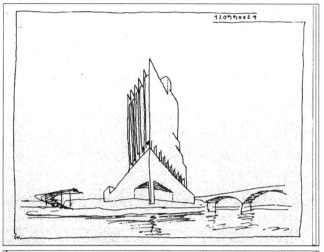

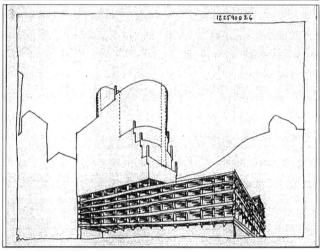

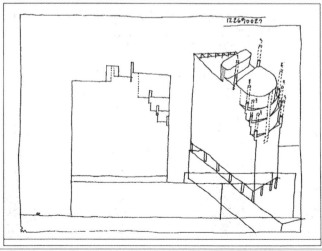

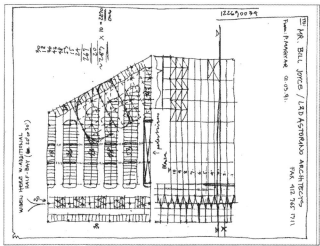

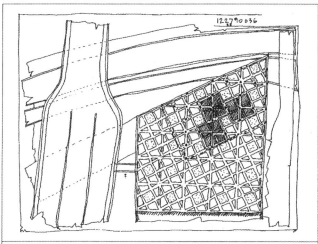

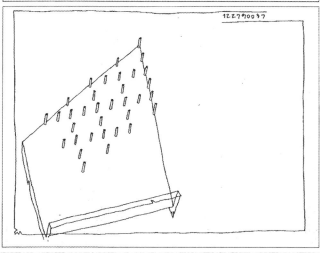

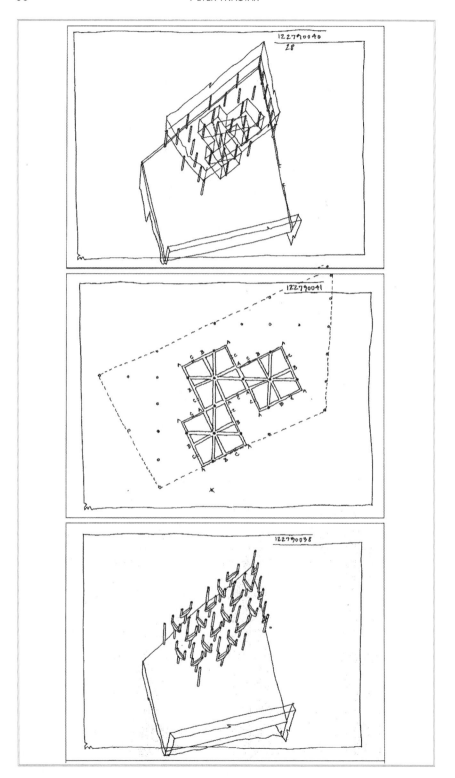

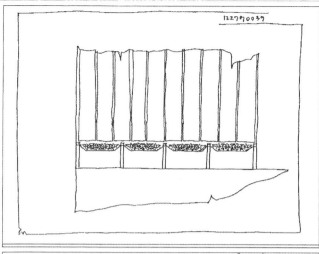

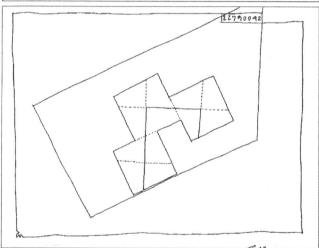

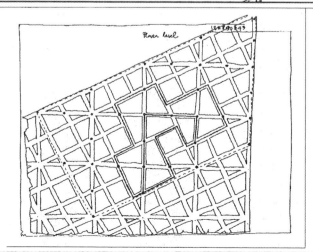

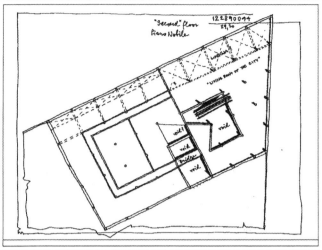

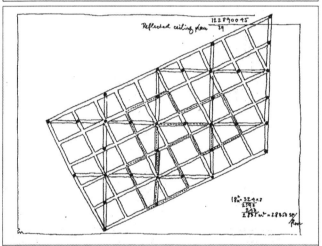

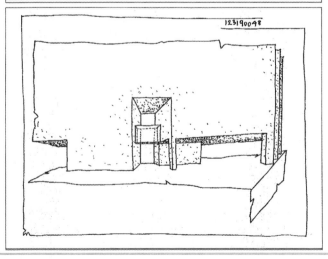

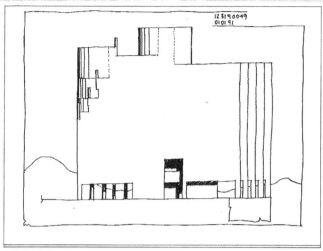

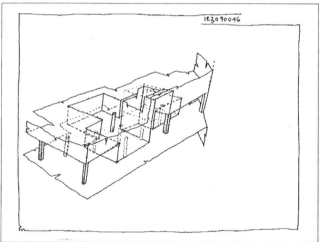

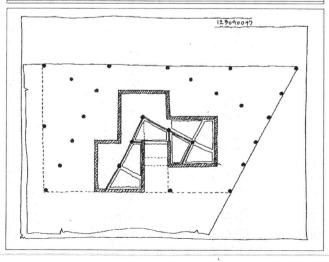

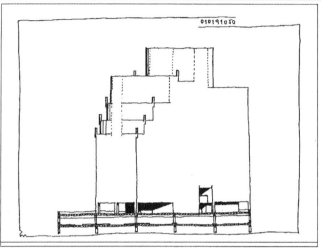

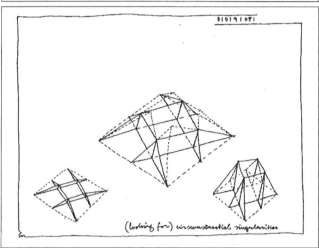

(looking for) circumstantial singularities

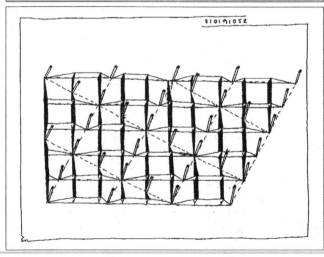

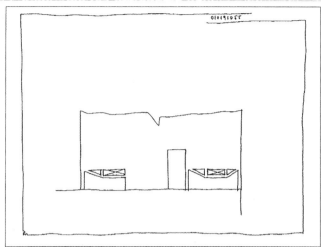

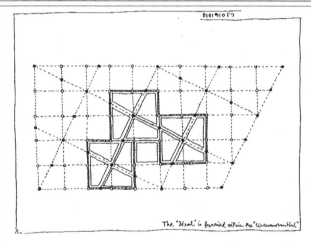

The "Ideal" is buried within the "circumstantial"

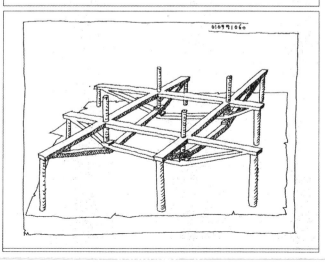

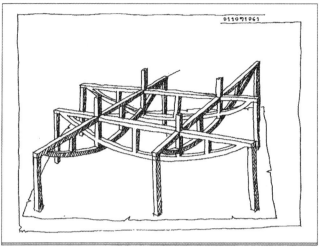

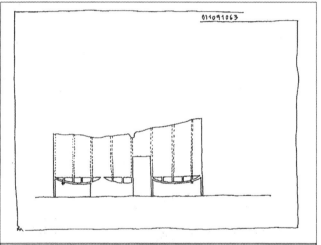

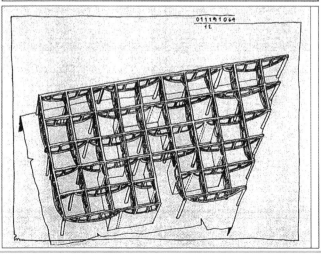

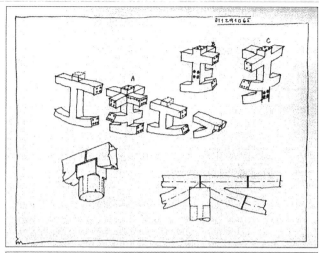

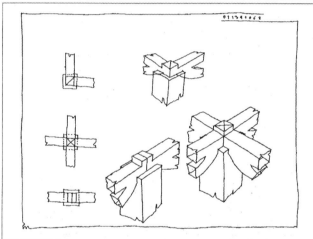

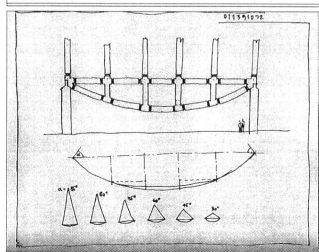

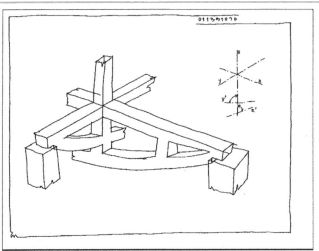

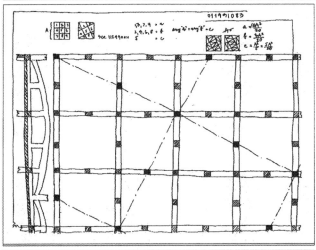

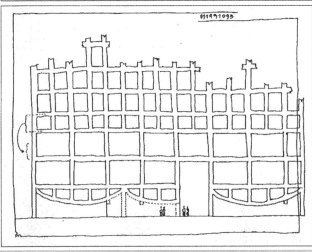

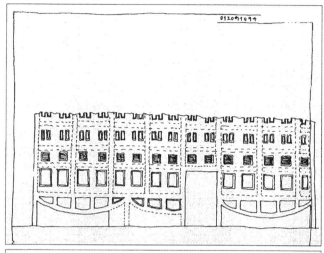

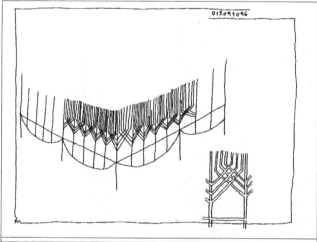

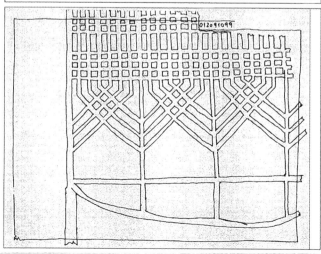

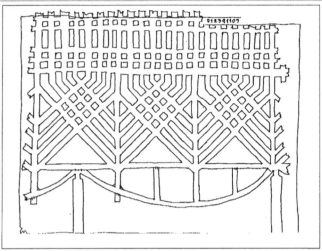

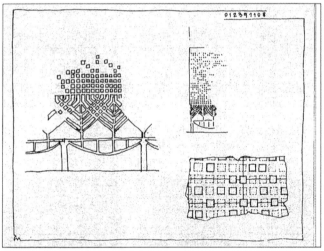

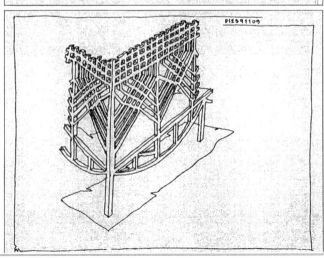

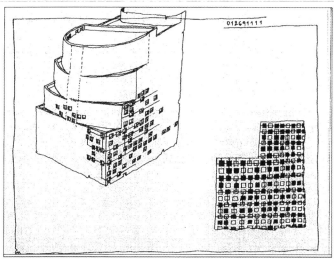

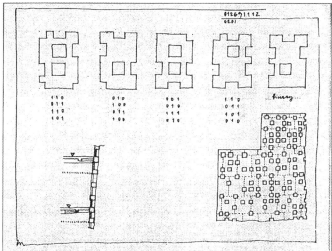

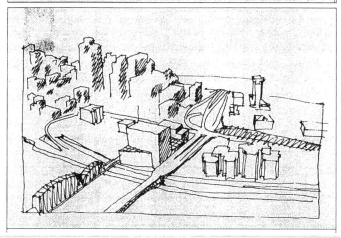

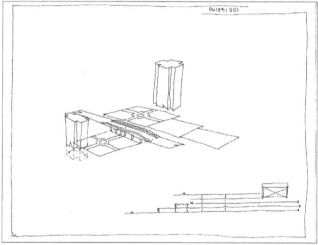

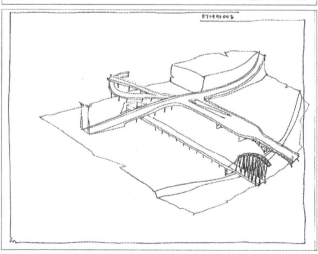

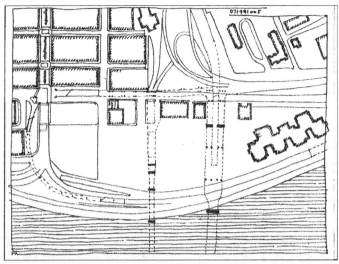

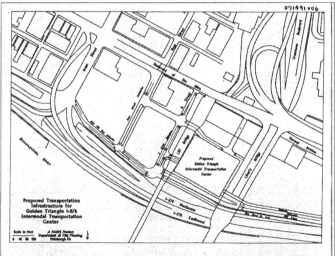

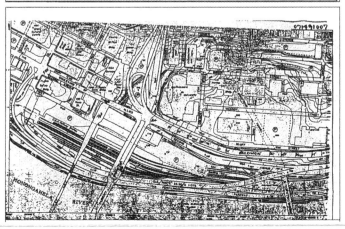

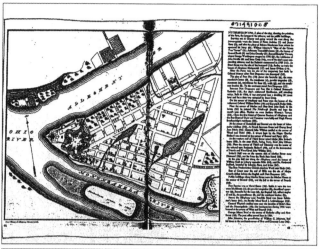

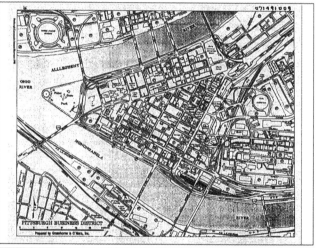

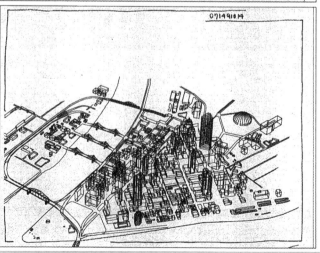

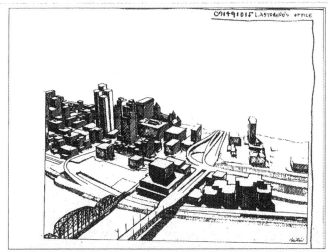

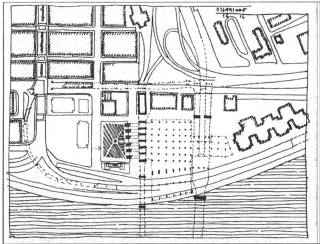

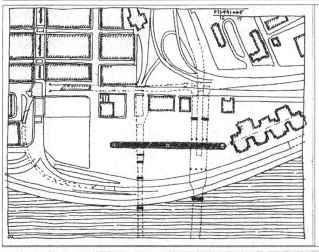

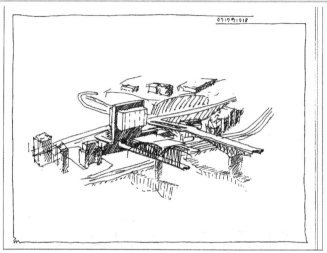

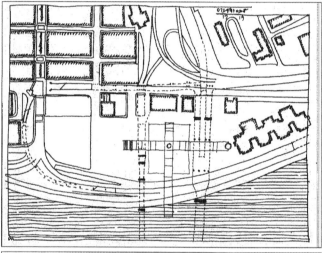

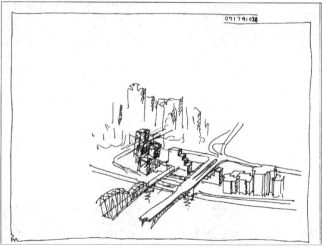

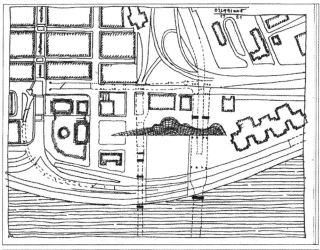

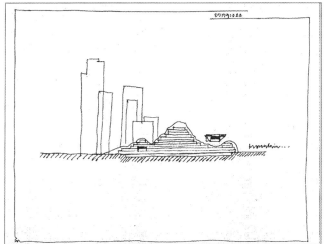

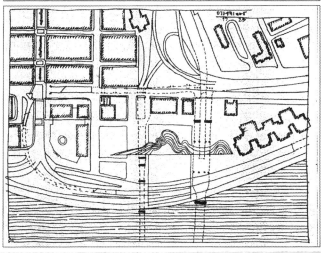

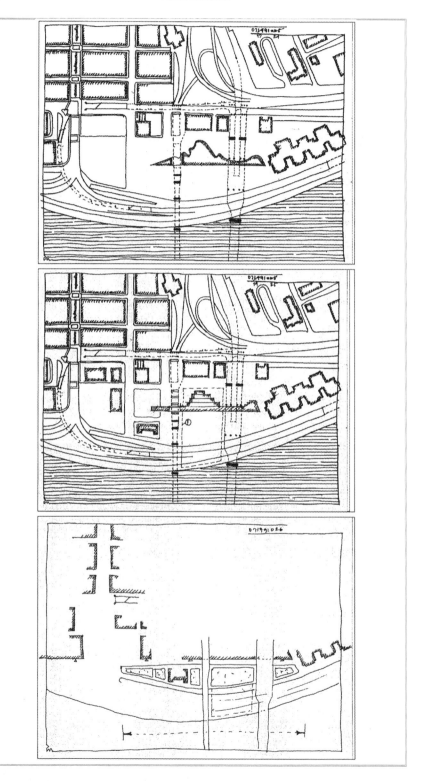

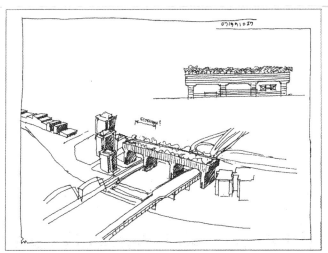

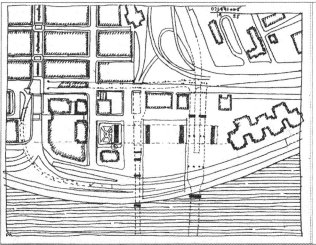

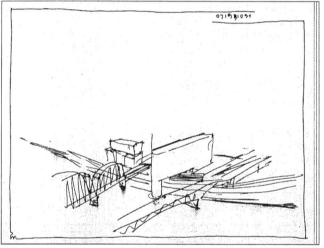

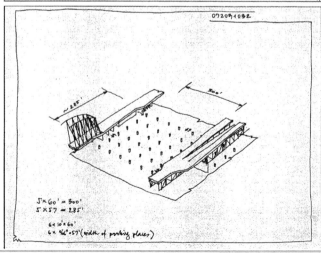

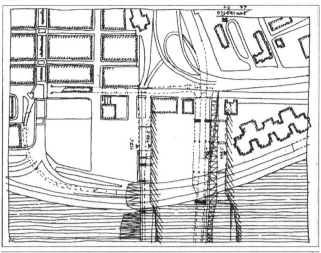

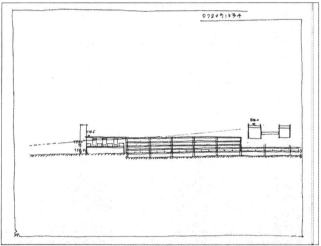

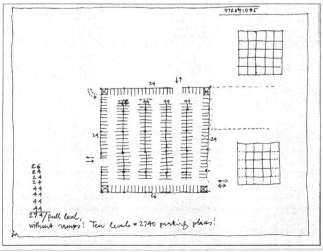

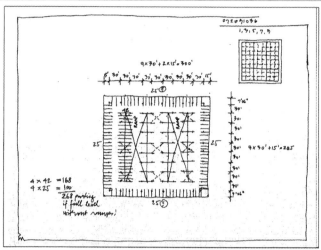

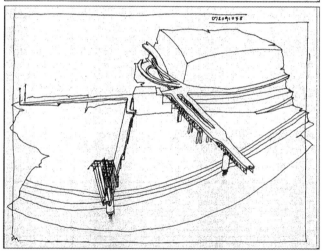

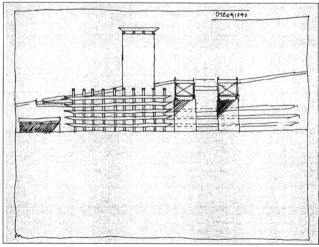

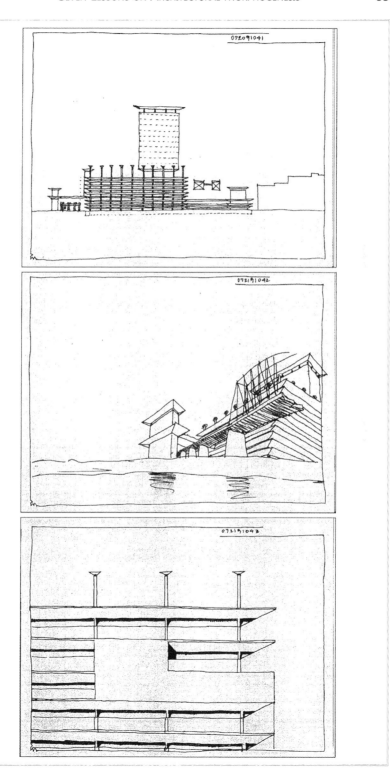

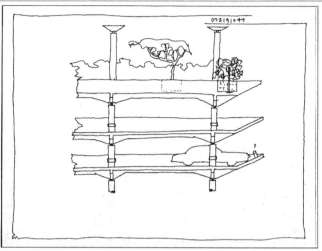

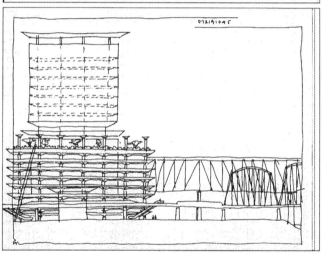

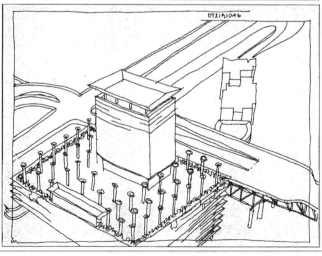

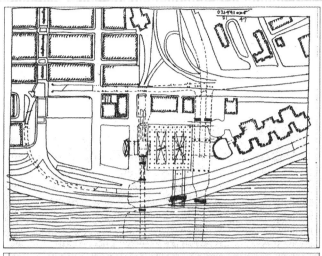

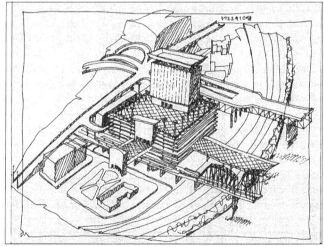

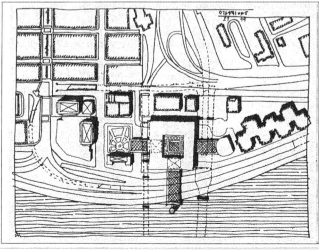

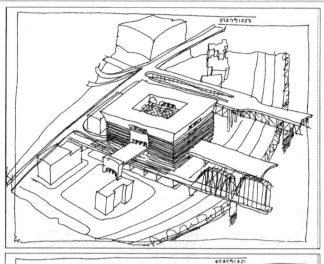

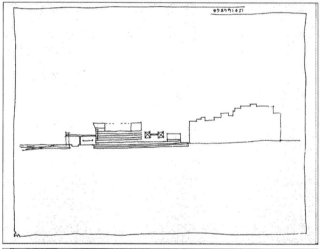

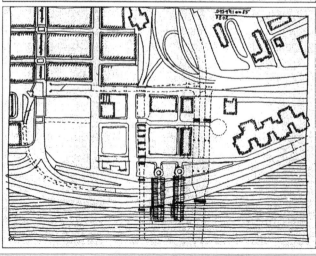

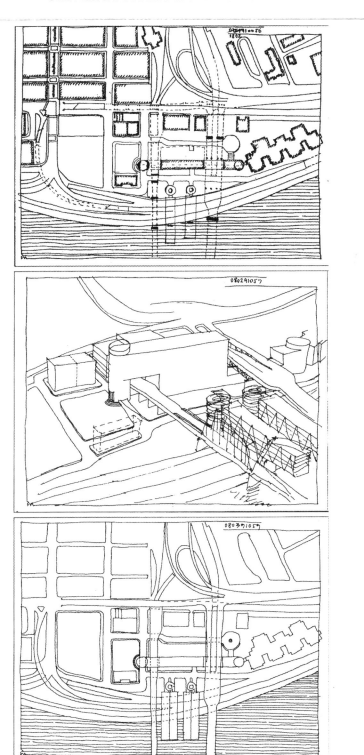

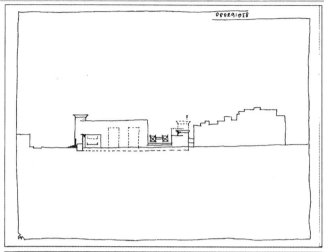

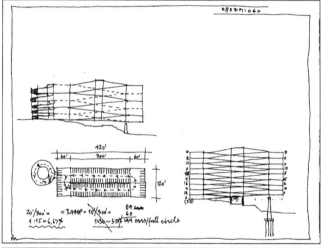

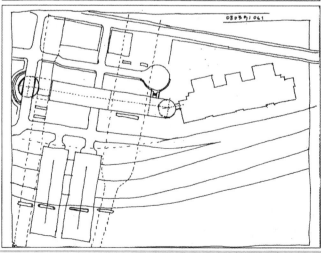

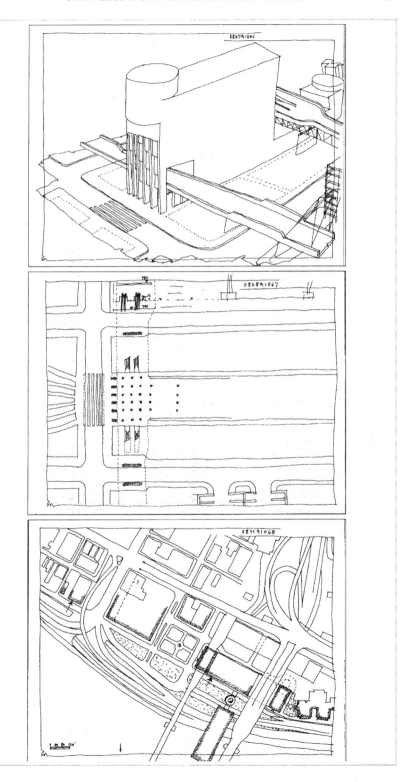

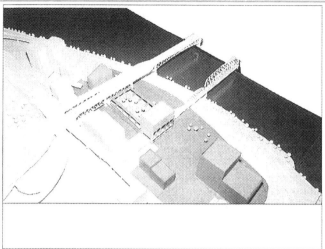

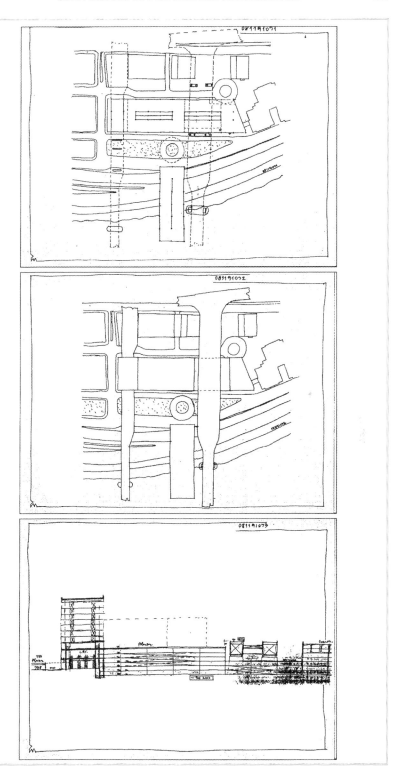

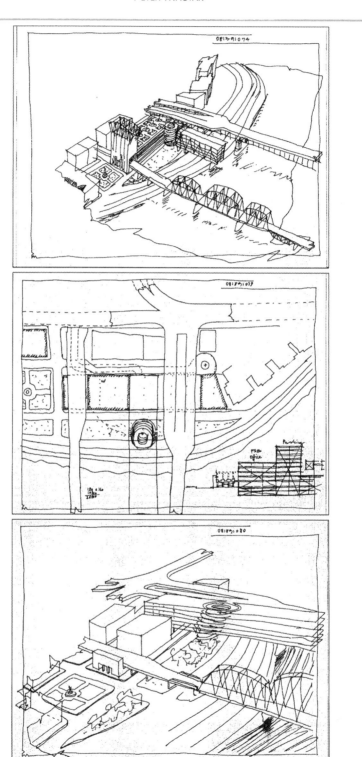

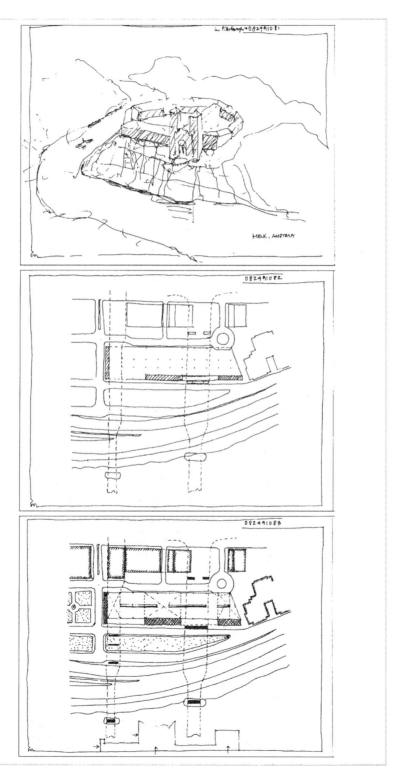

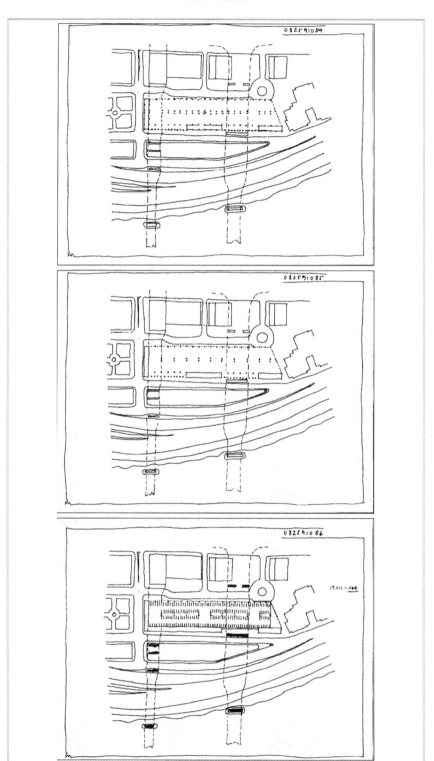

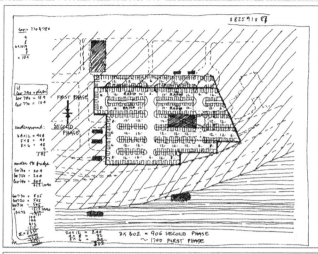

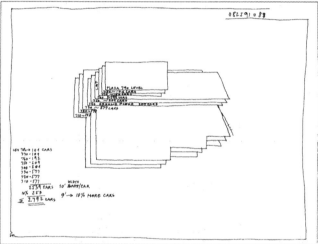

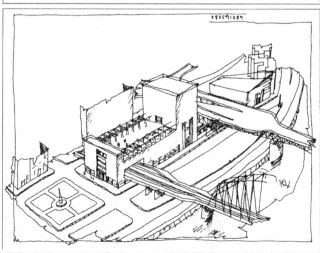

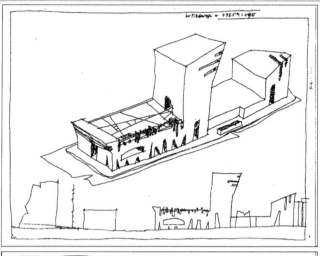

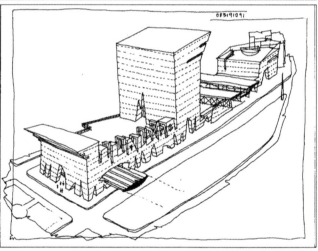

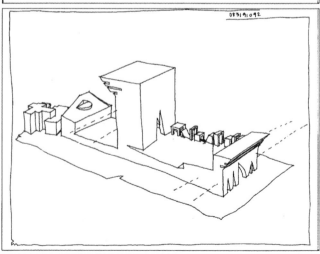

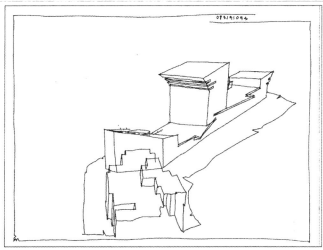

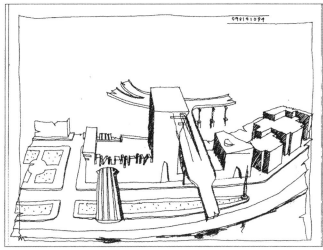

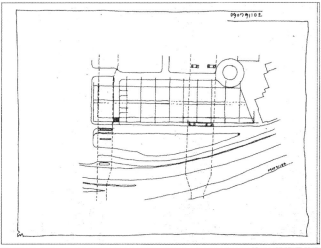

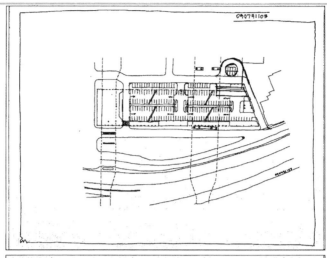

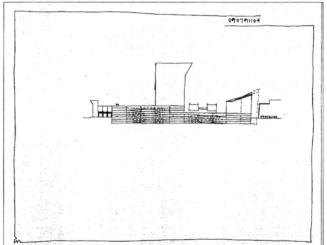

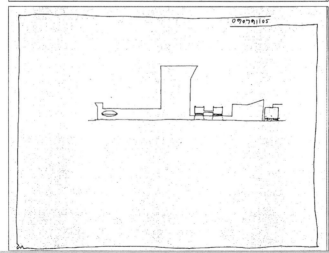

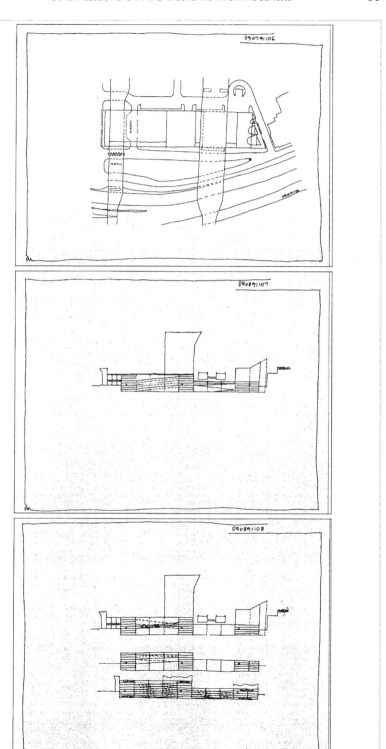

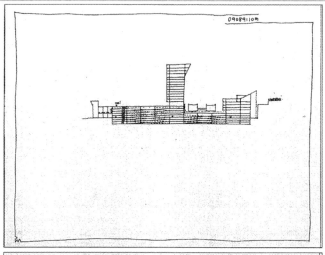

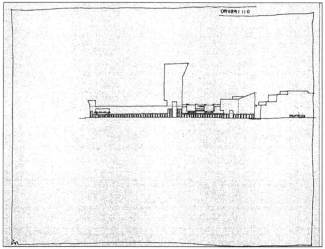

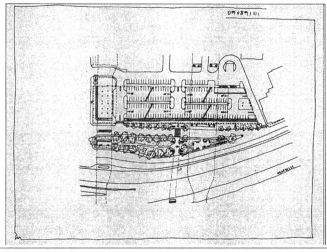

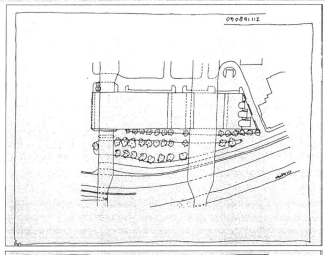

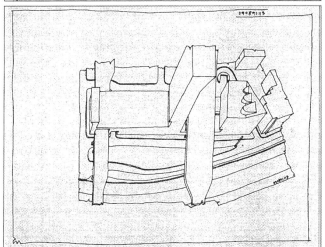

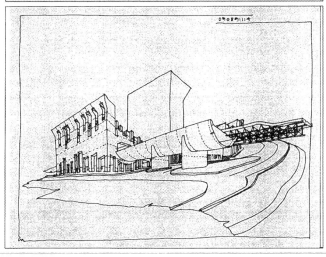

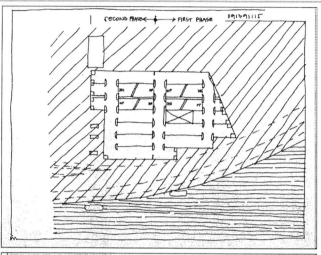

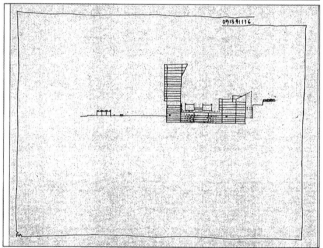

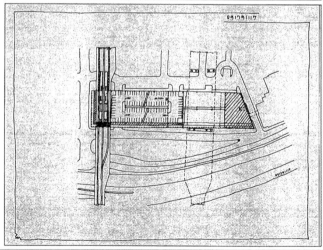

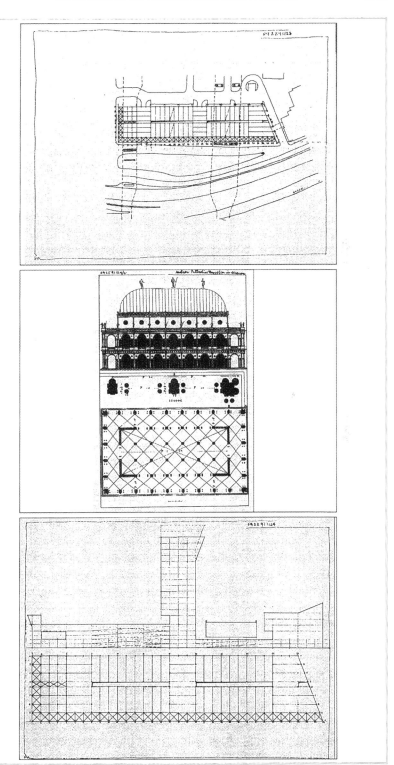

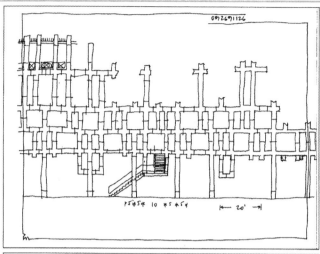

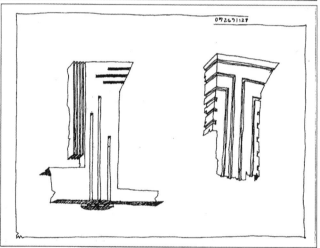

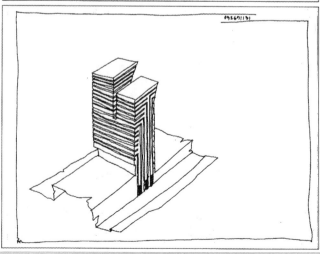

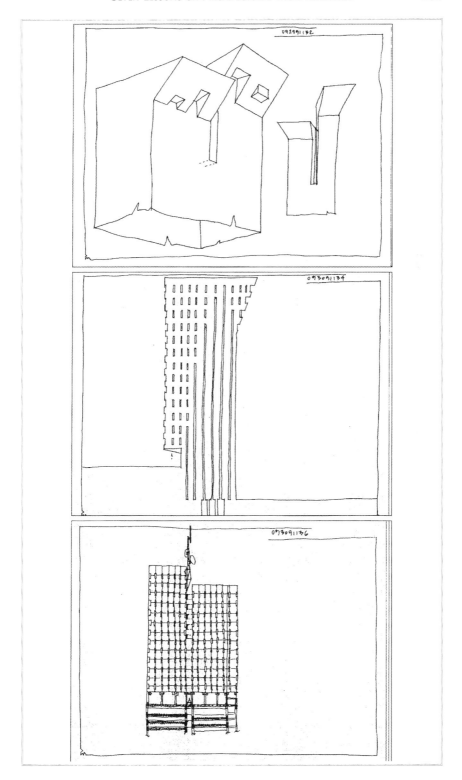

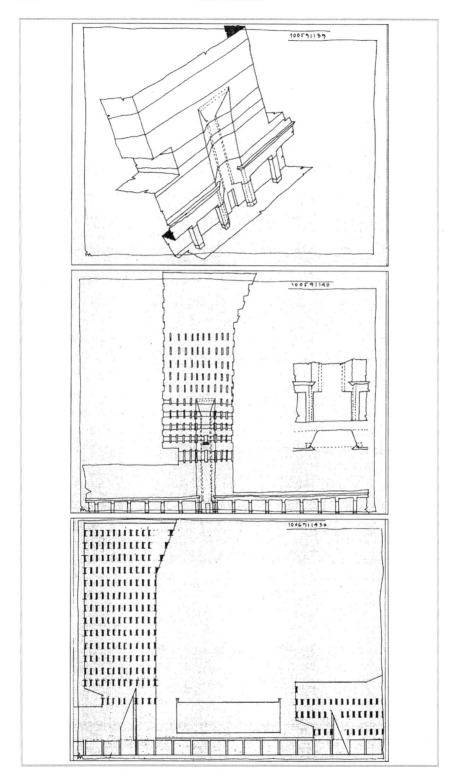

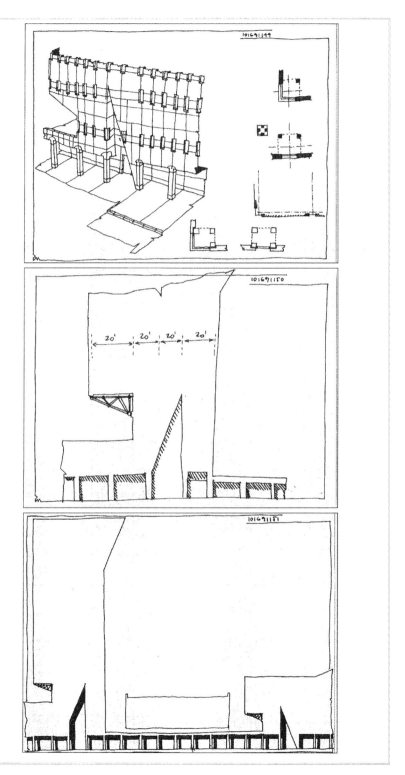

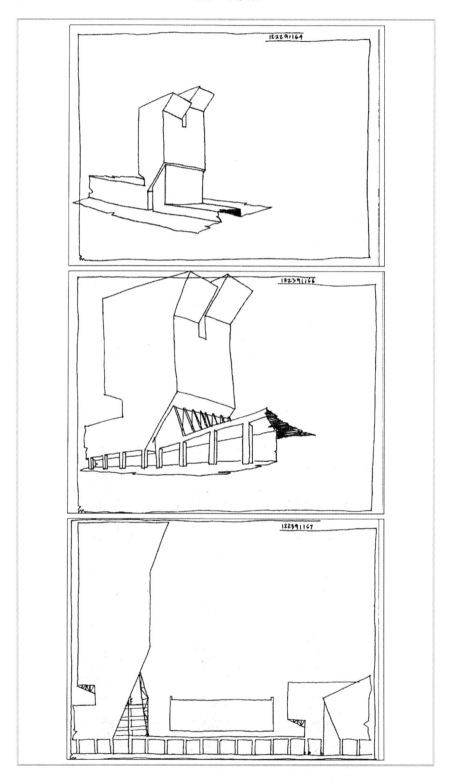

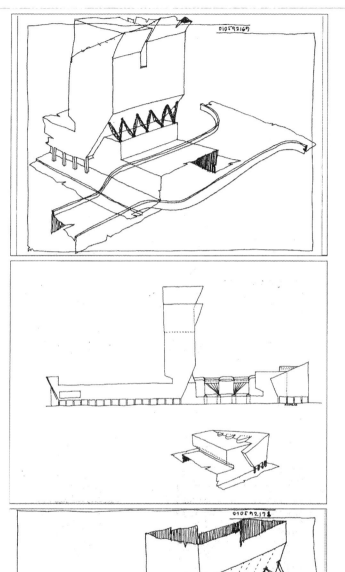

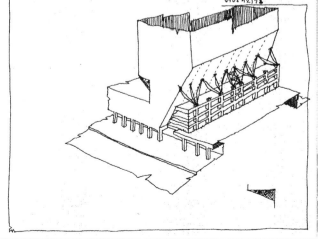

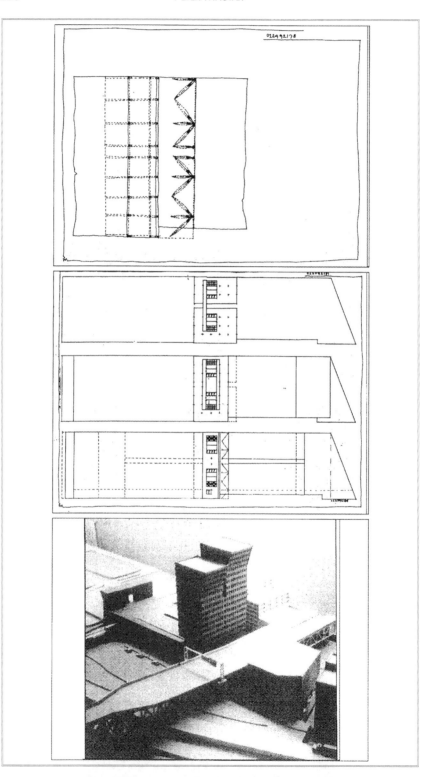

YOKOHAMA INTERNATIONAL PORT

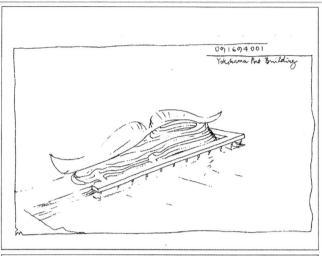

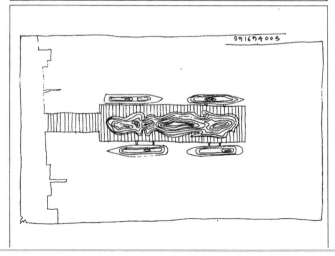

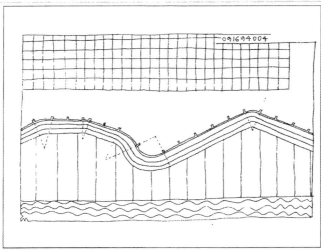

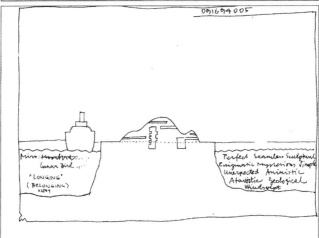

YOKOHAMA IN 1872

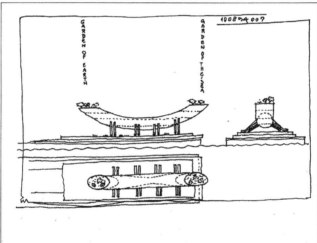

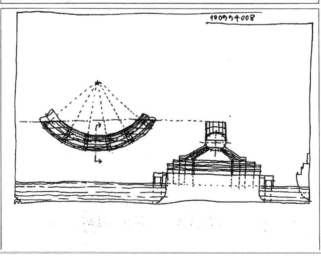

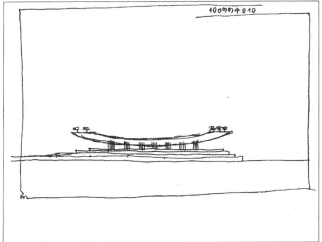

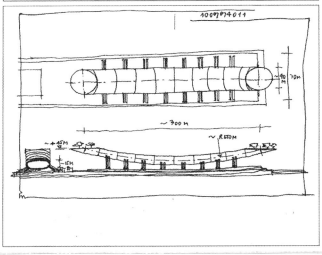

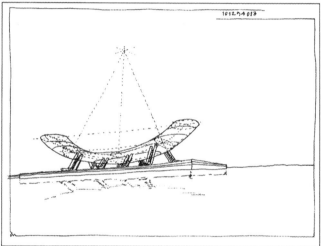

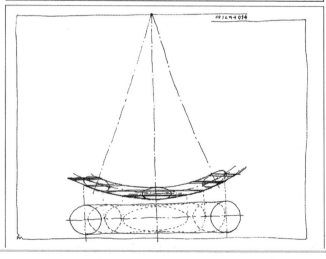

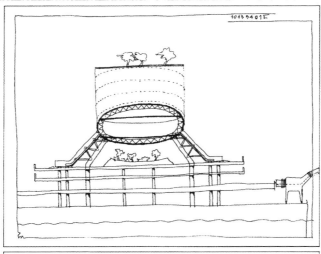

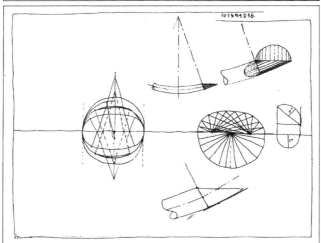

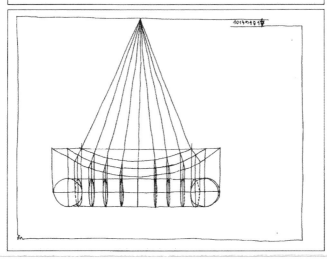

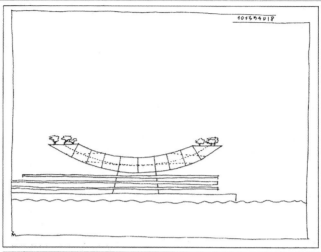

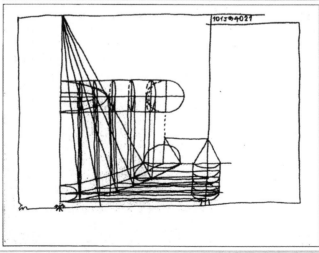

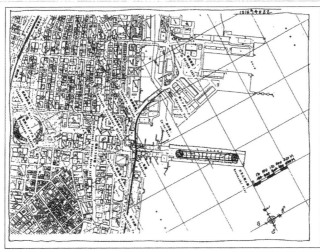

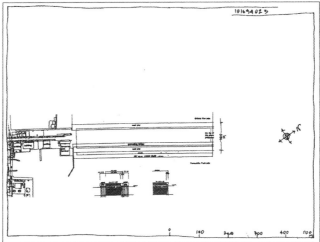

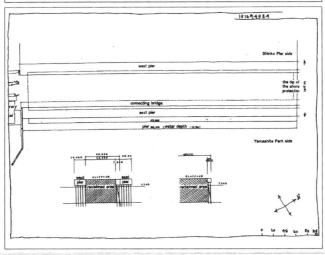

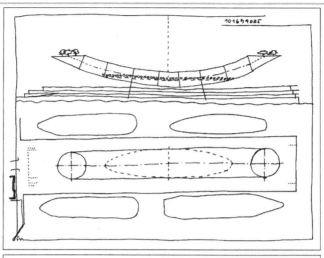

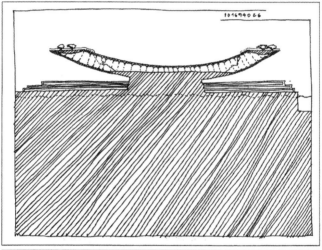

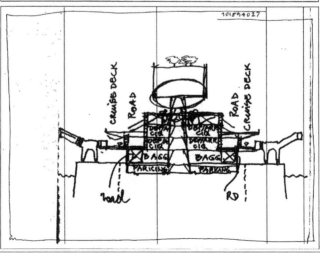

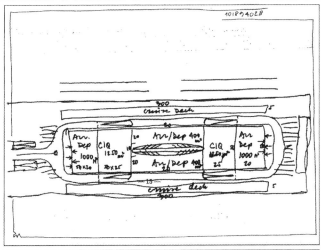

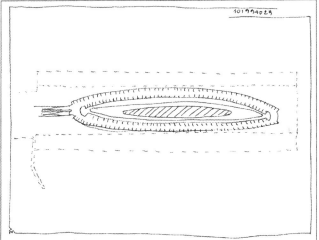

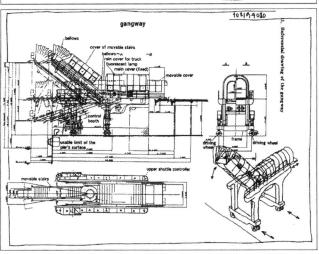

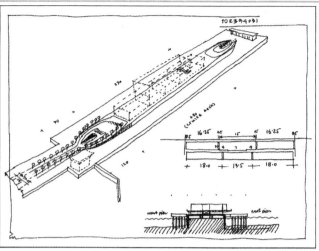

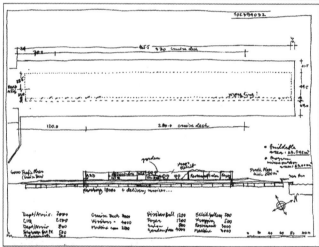

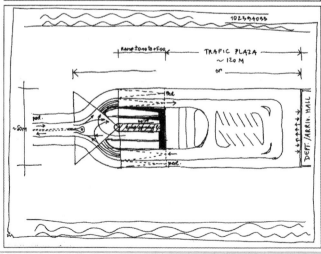

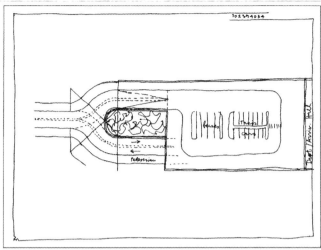

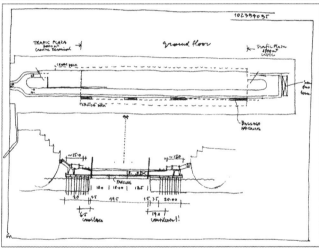

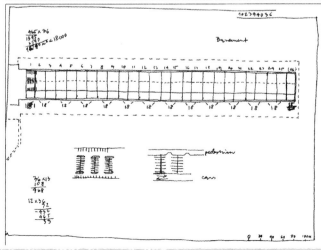

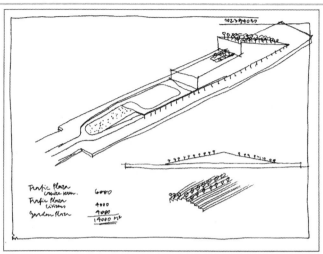

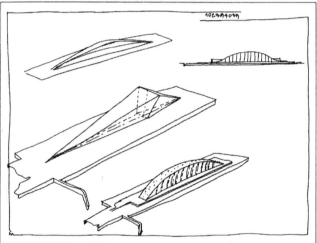

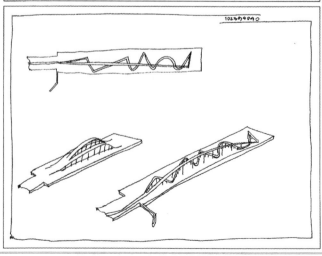

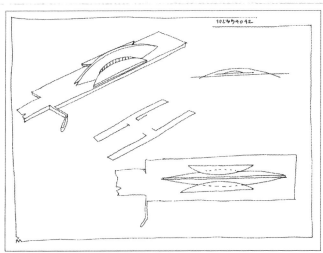

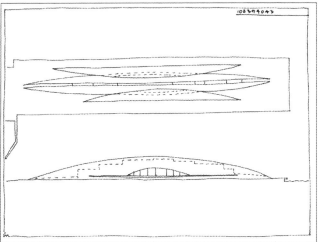

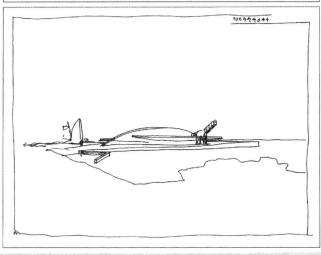

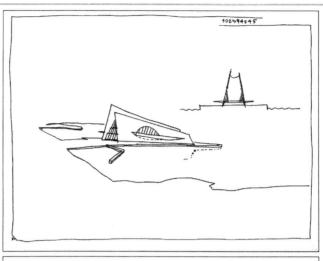

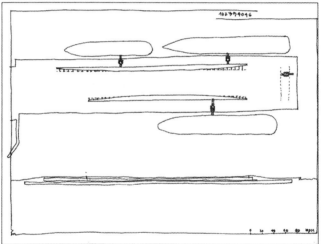

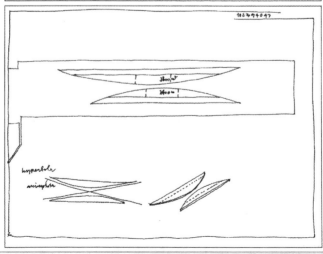

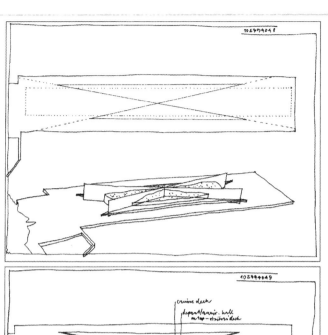

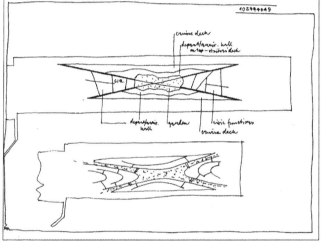

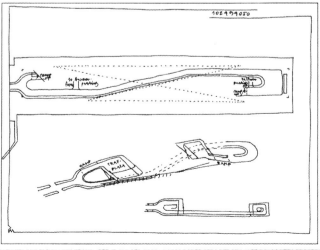

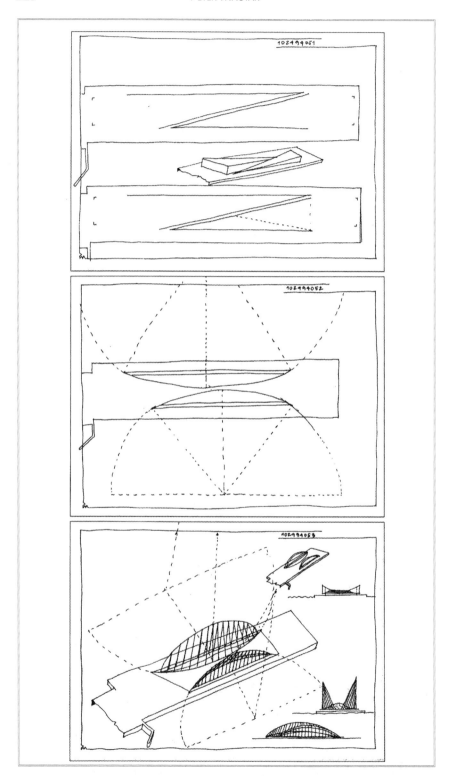

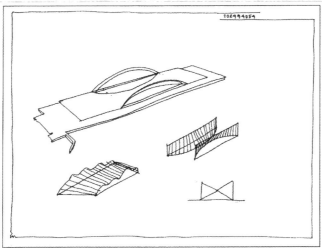

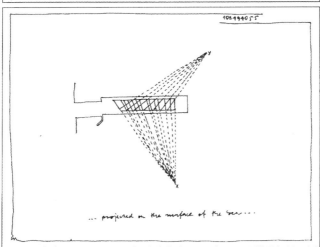

... projected on the surface of the sea ...

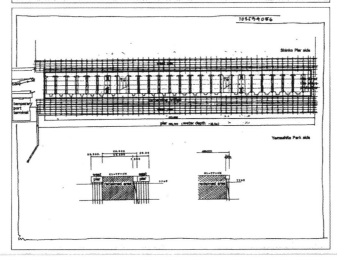

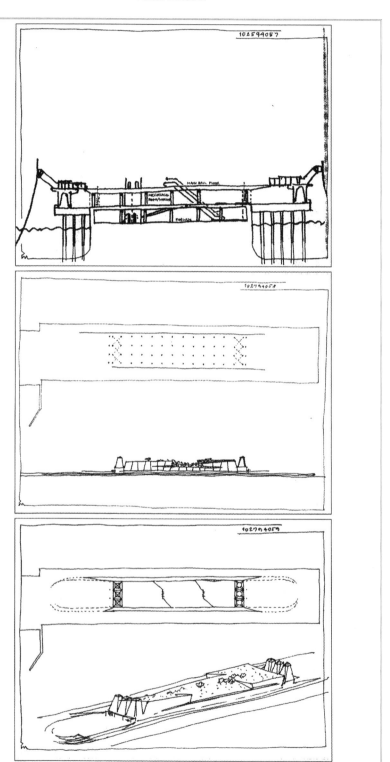

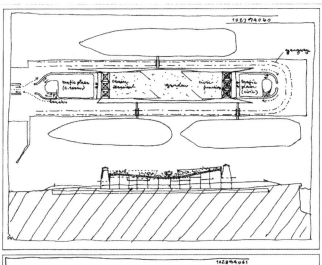

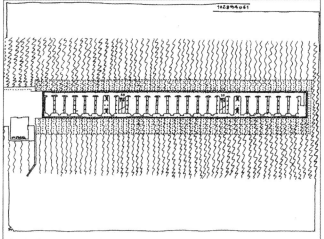

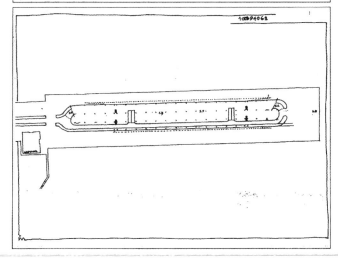

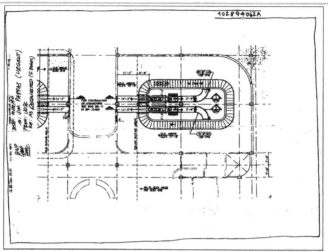

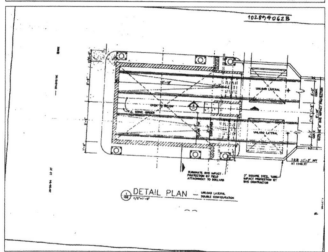

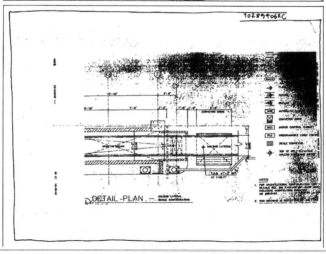

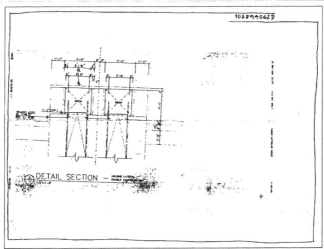

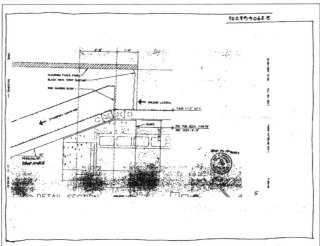

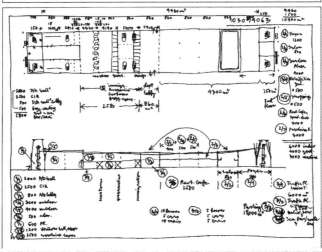

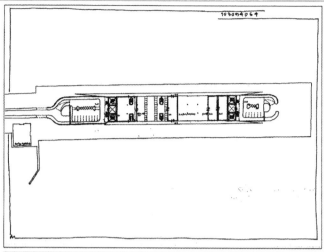

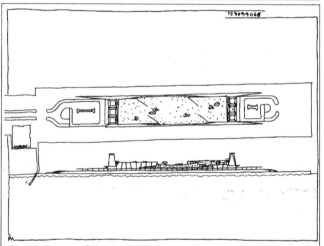

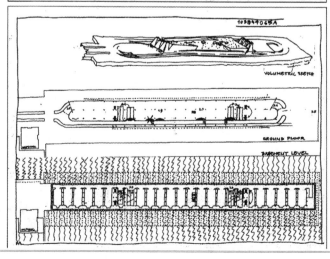

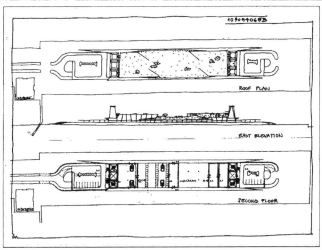

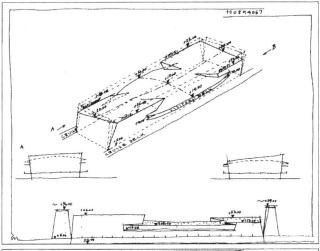

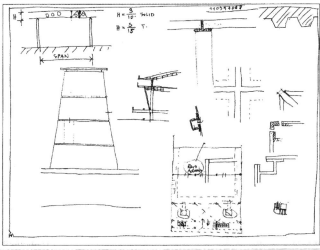

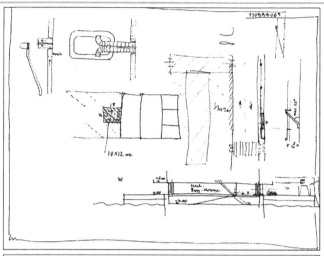

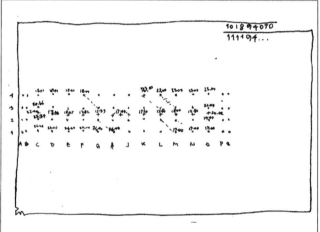

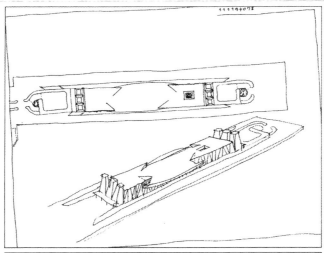

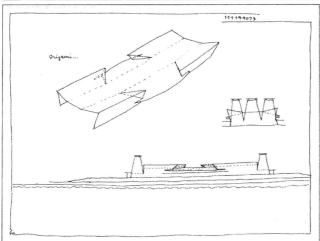

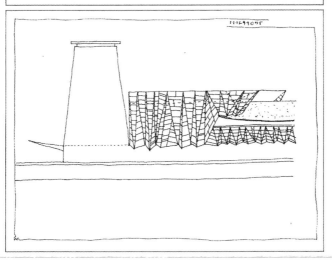

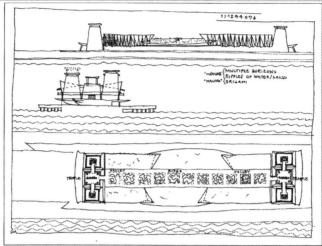

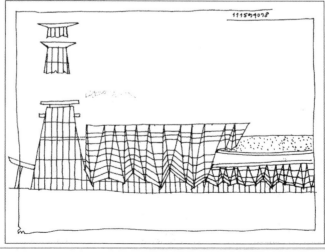

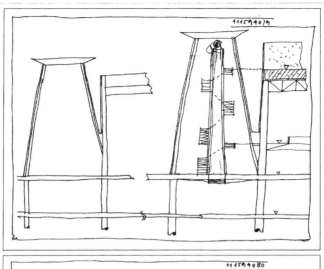

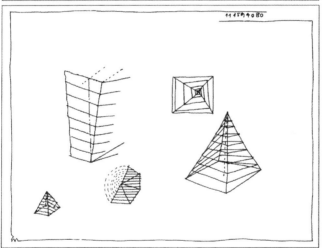

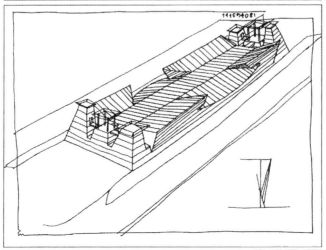

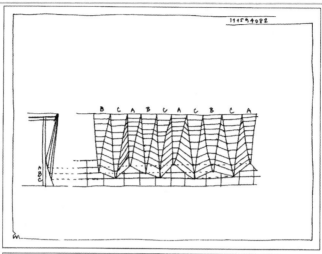

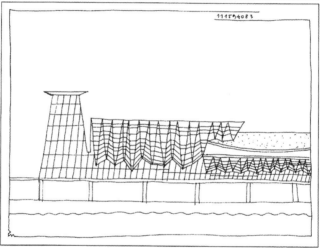

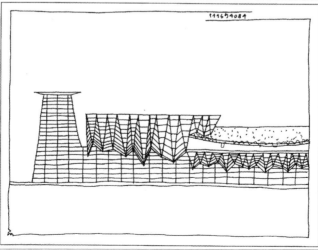

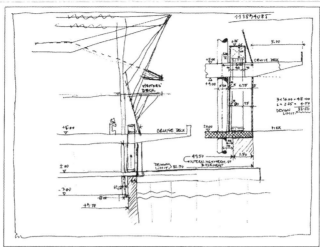

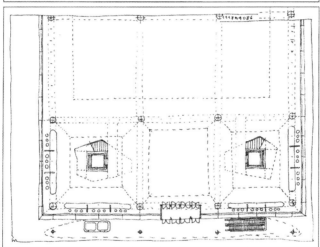

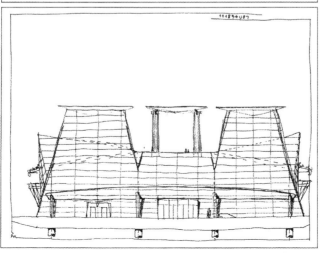

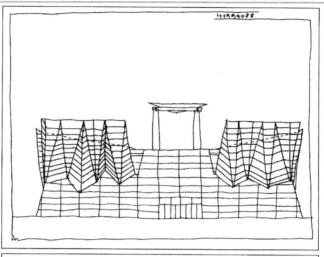

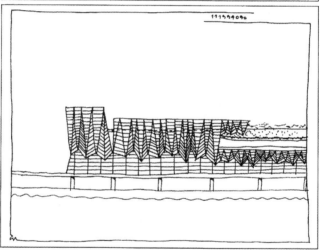

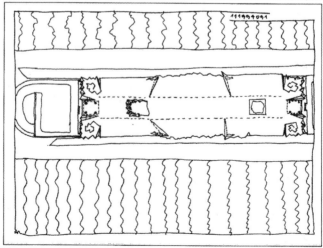

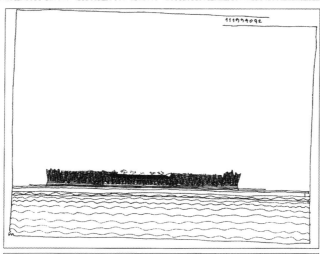

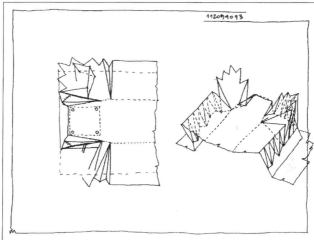

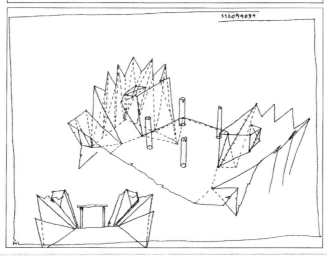

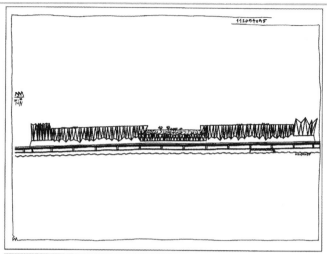

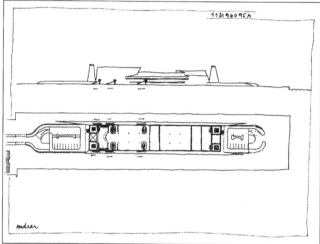

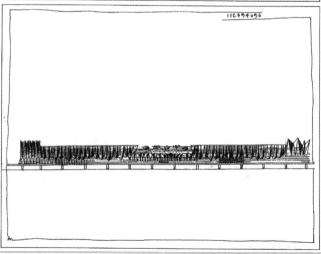

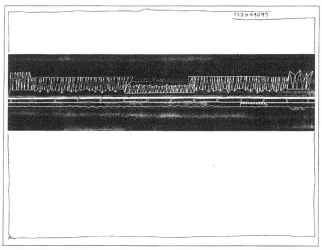

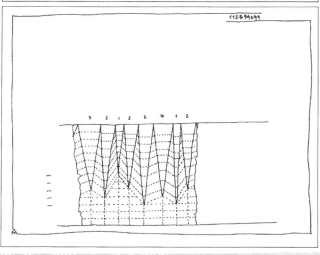

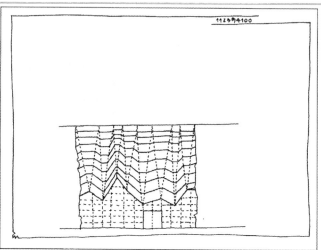

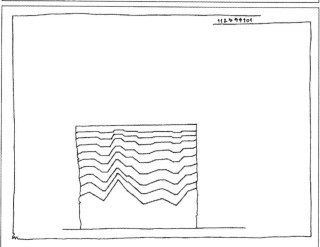

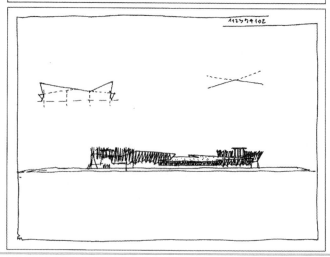

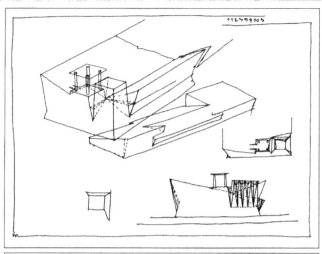

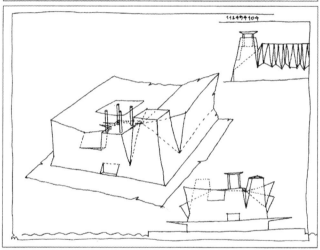

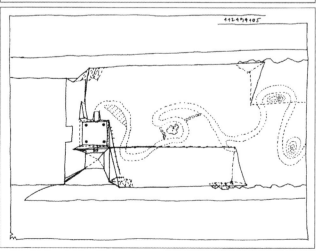

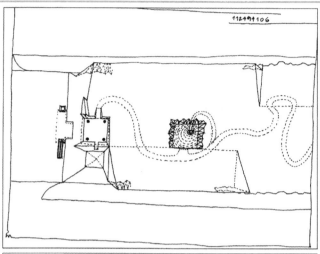

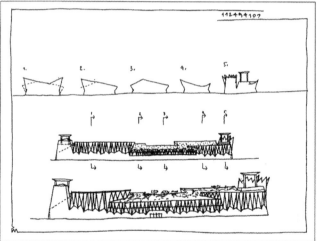

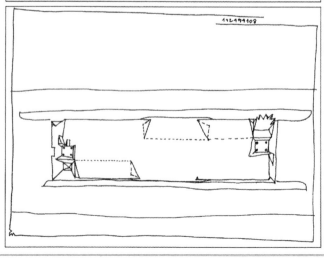

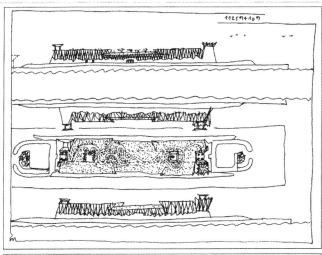

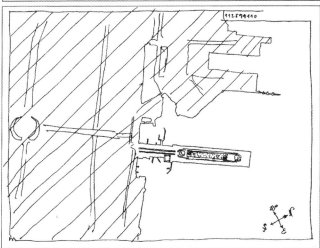

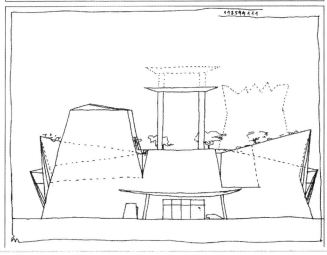

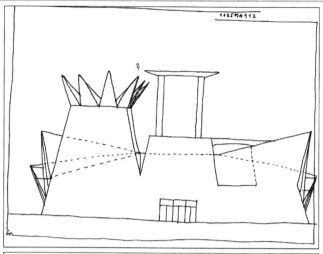

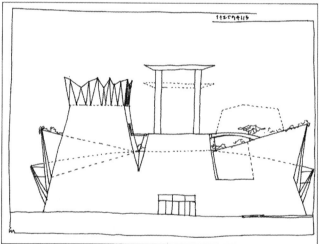

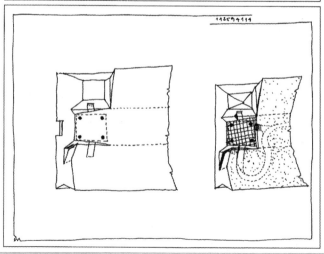

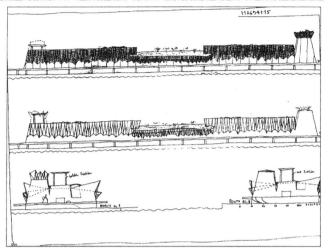

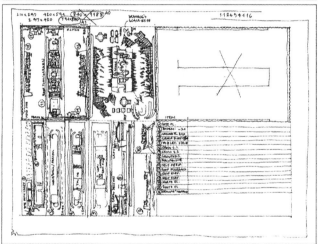

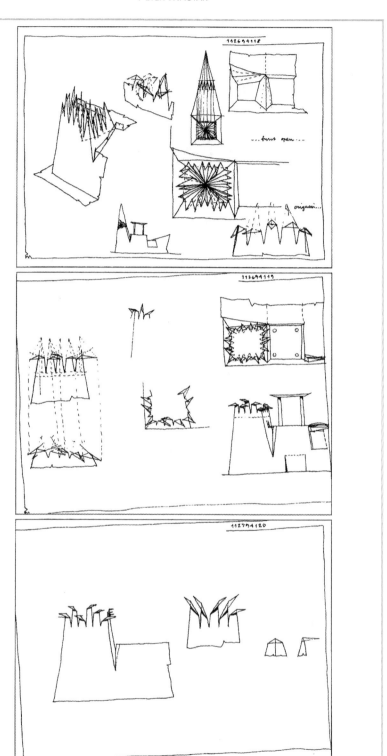

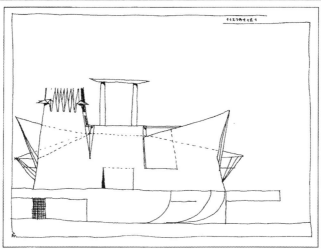

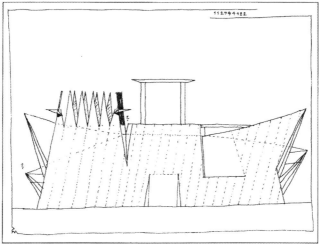

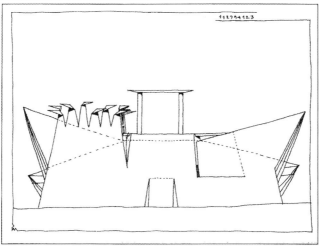

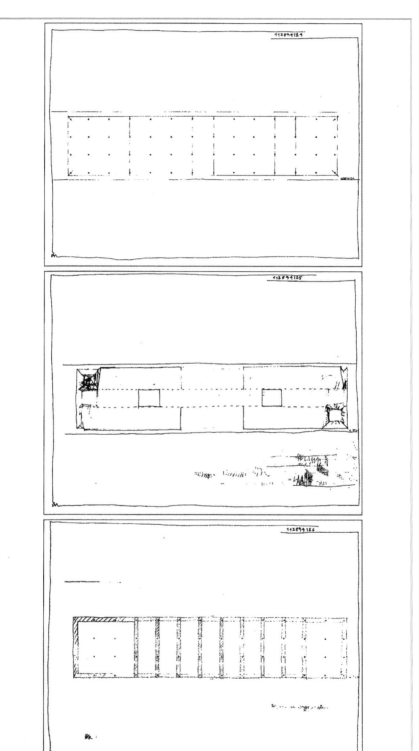

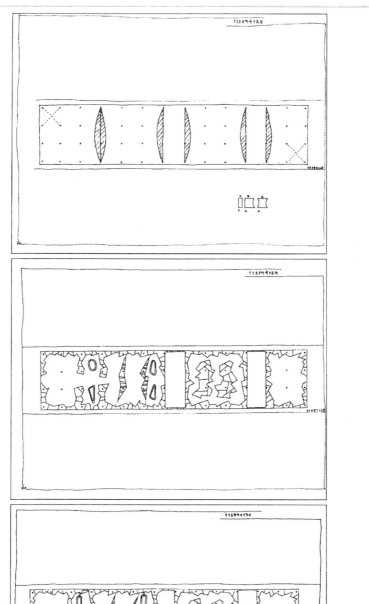

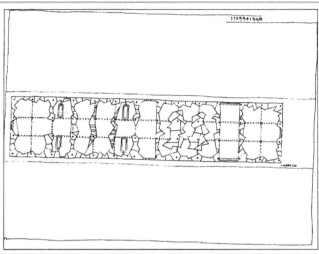

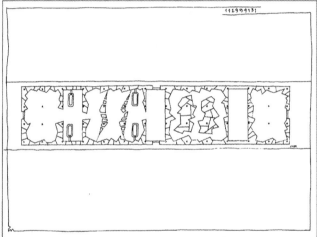

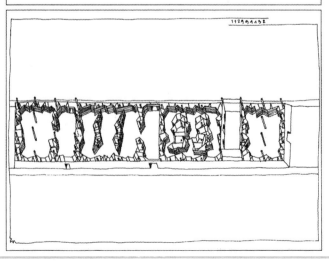

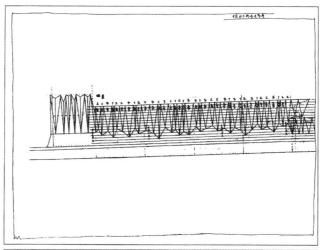

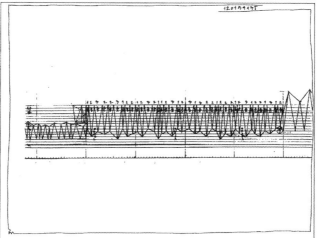

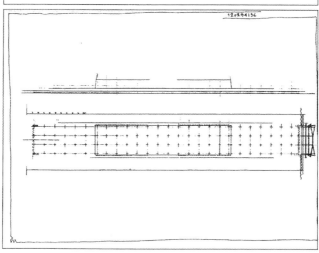

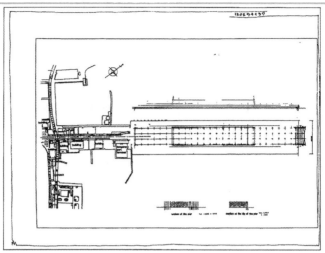

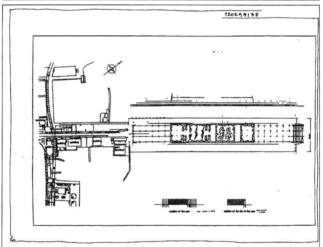

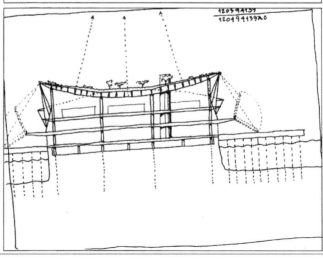

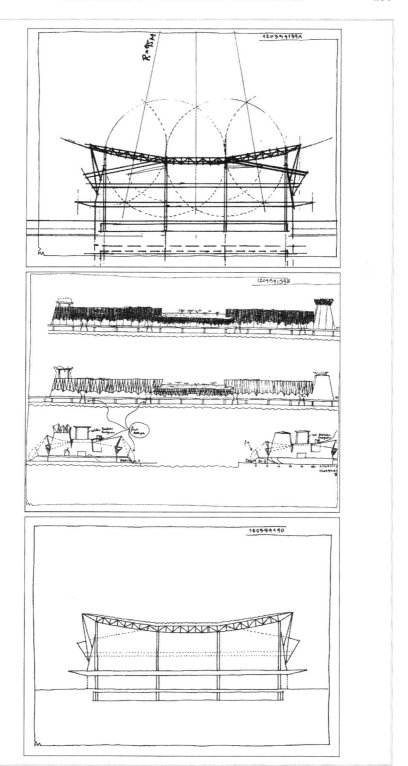

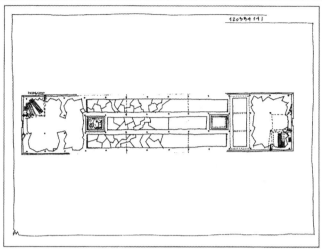

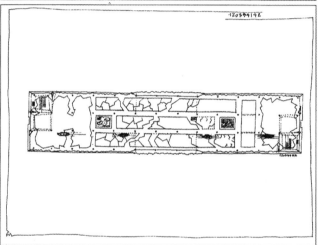

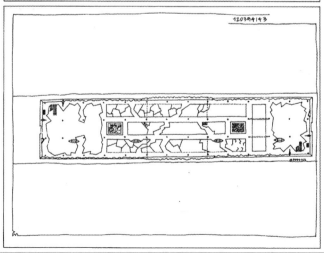

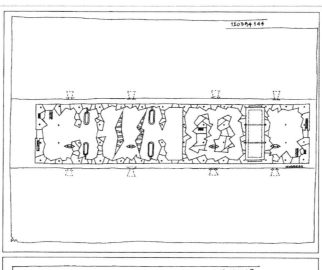

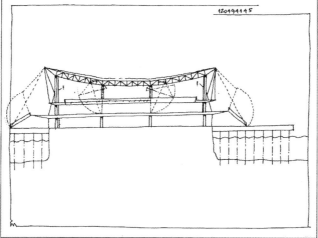

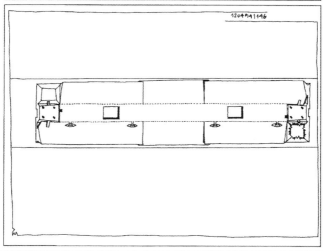

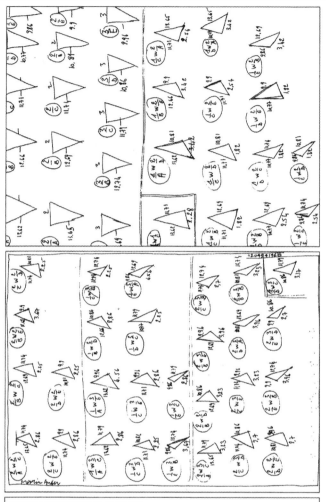

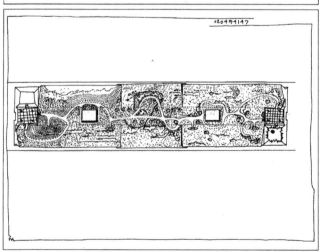

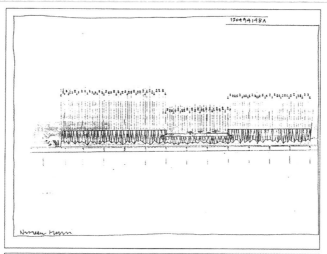

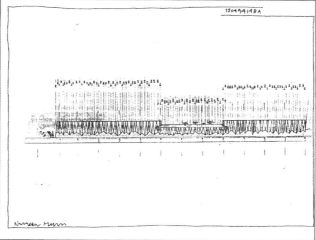

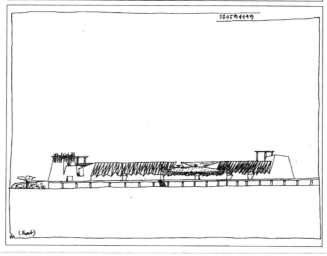

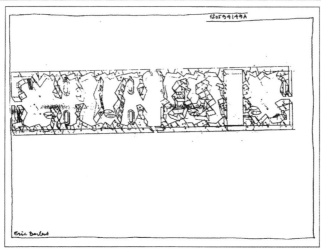

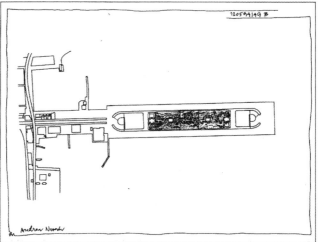

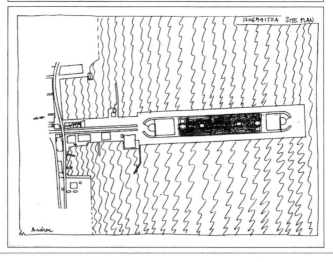

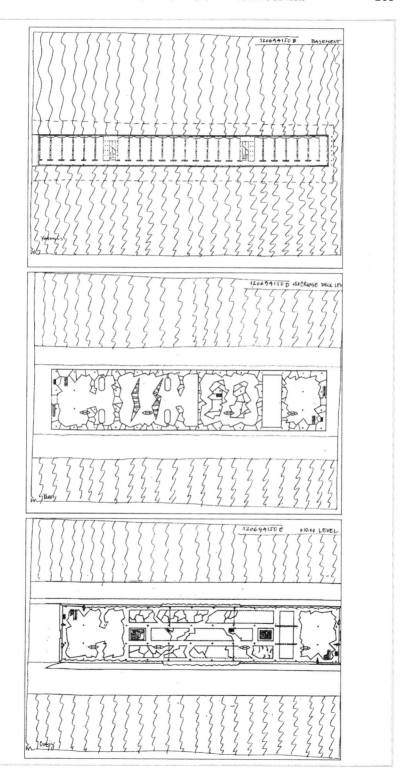

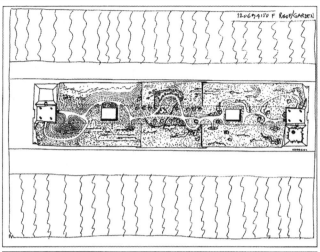

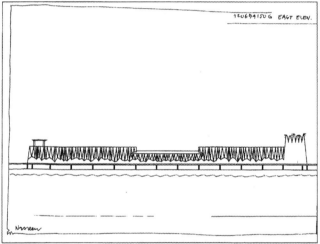

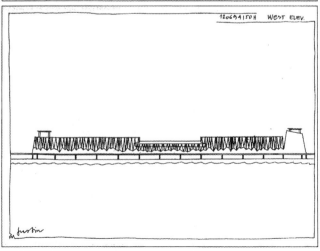

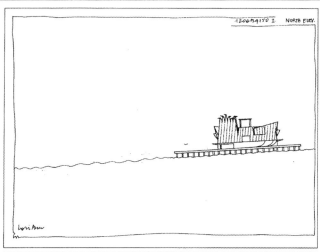

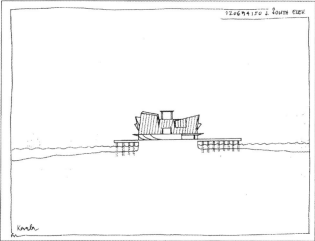

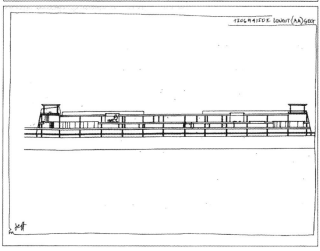

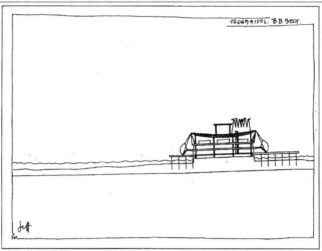

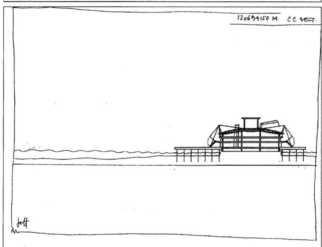

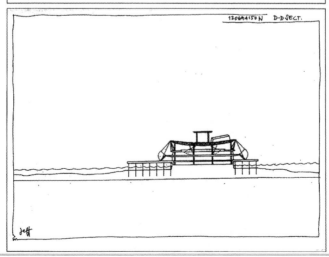

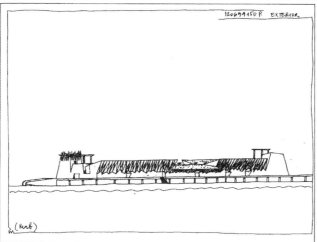

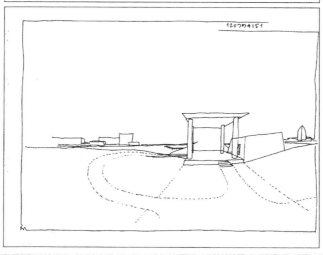

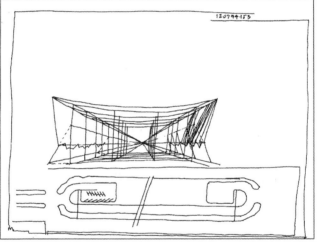

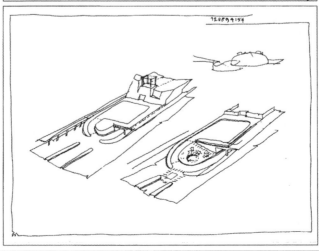

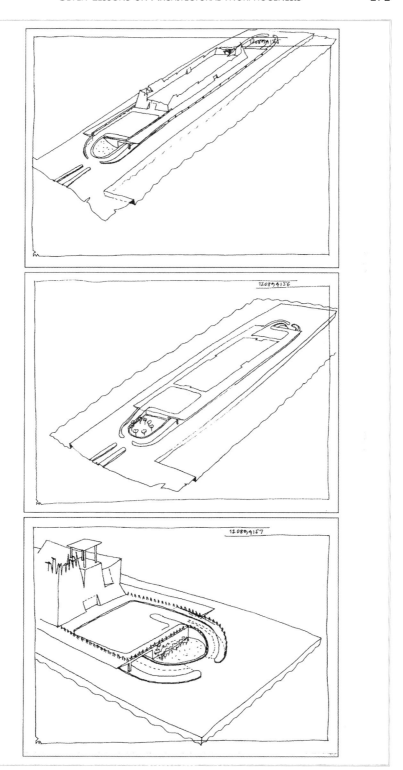

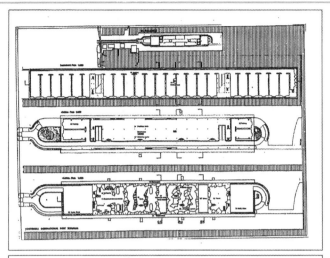

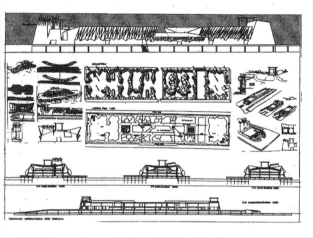

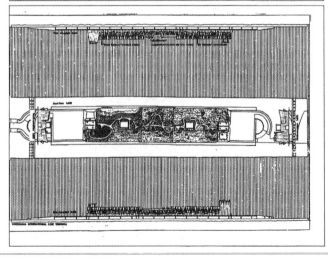

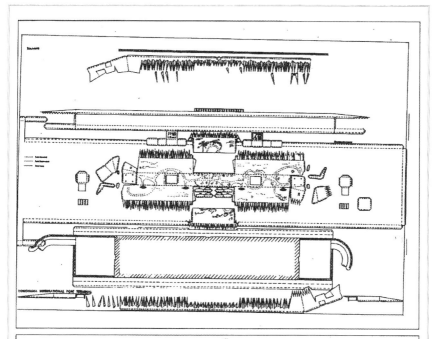

横浜港国際客船ターミナル国際建築設計競技
YOKOHAMA INTERNATIONAL PORT TERMINAL DESIGN COMPETITION

作品受領書
R e c e i p t

受 録 者 氏 名 Name of Registrant	PETER MAGYAR
受 録 番 号 Registration No.	2 4 0 3
受 領 年 月 日 Receipt of Date	

設計競技規作品を受領しました。
We received and registered your Plan.

横浜港国際客船ターミナル国際建築設計競技事務局
〒 231 横浜市中区山下町 2 番地 産業貿易センタービル 横浜市港湾局

YOKOHAMA INTERNATIONAL PORT TERMINAL DESIGN COMPETITION OFFICE
Port and Harbor Bureau, Yokohama City Office, Sangyoboeki-Center Bldg.
2 Yamashita-Cho, Naka-ku, Yokohama 231, Japan

Tel : 045-671-7350 Fax : 045-671-7399

NATIONAL THEATER 2 BUDAPEST

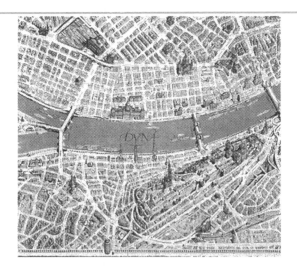

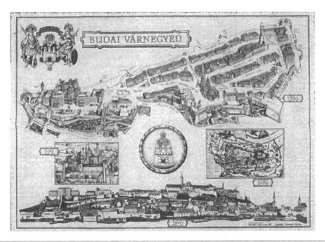

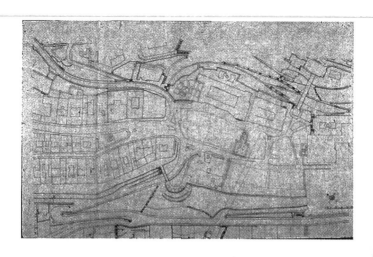

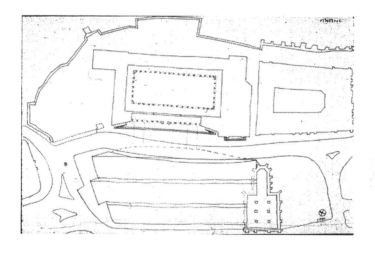

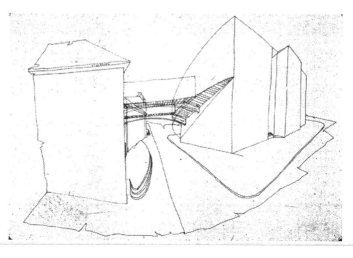

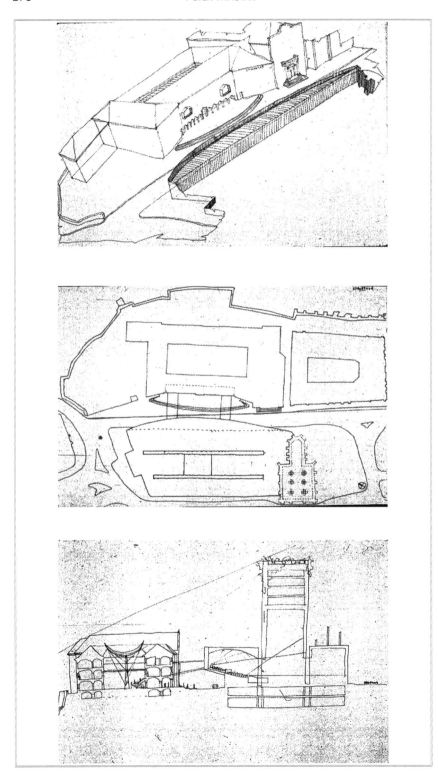

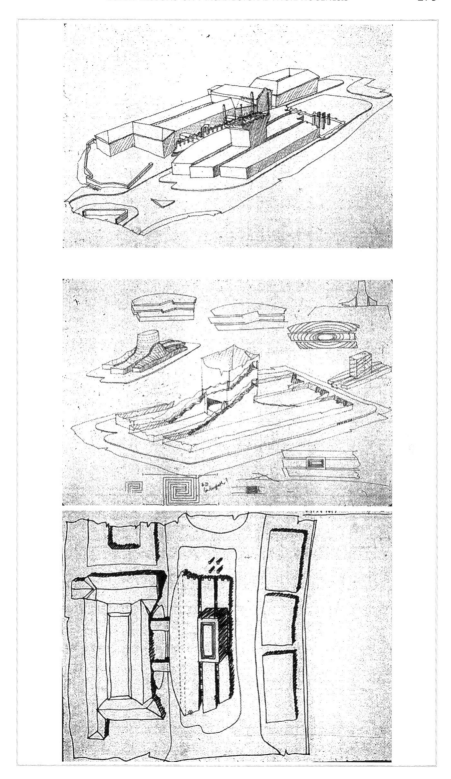

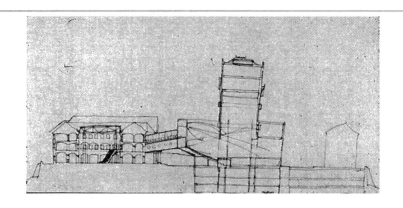

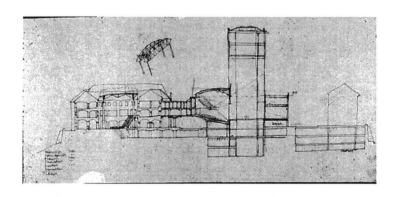

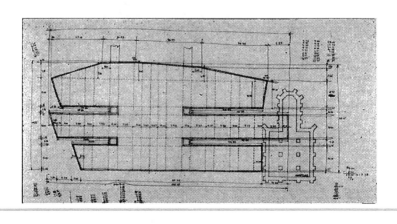

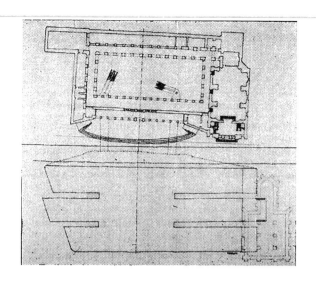

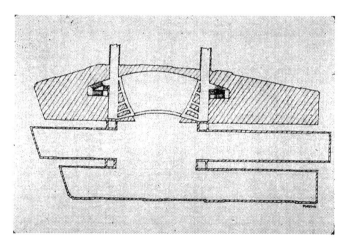

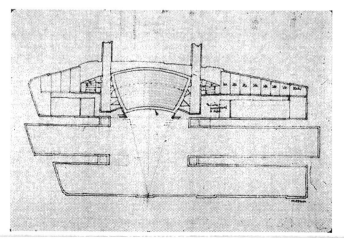

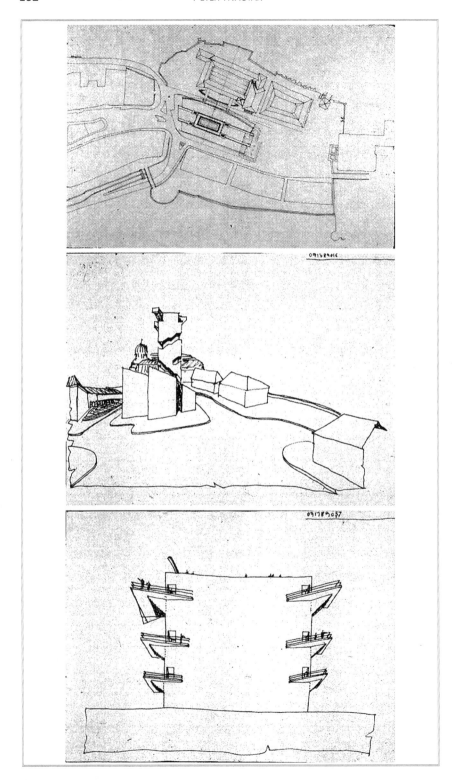

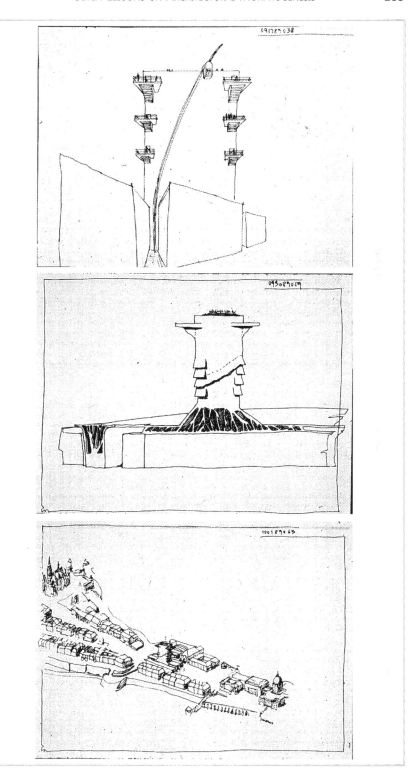

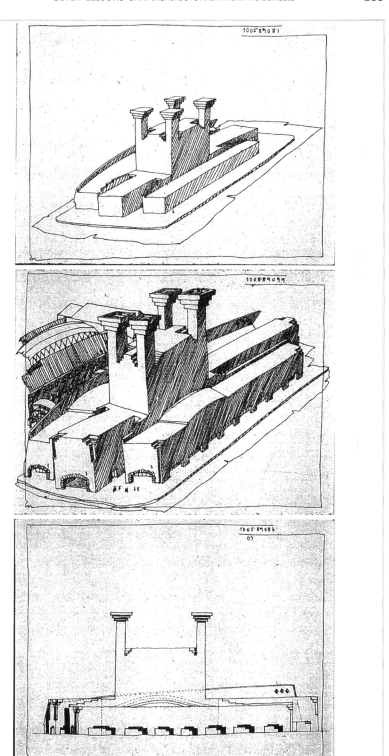

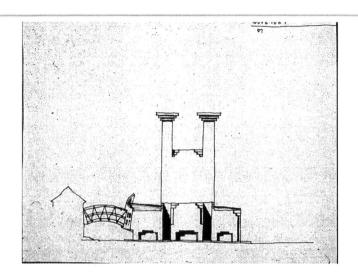

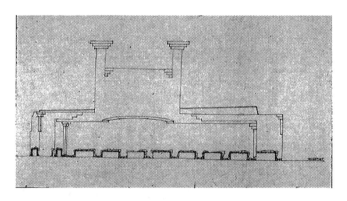

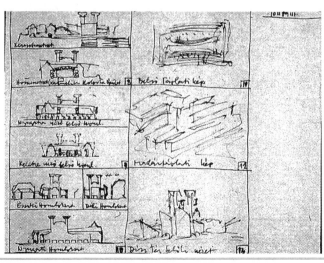

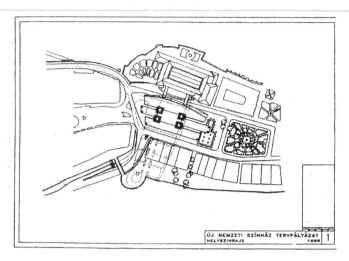

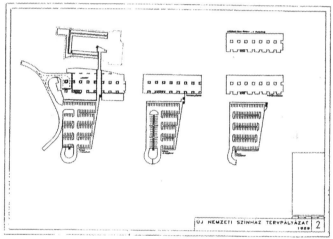

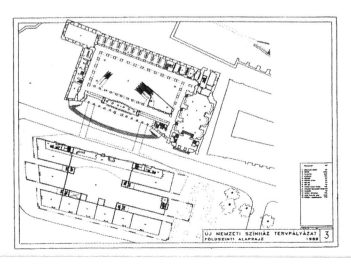

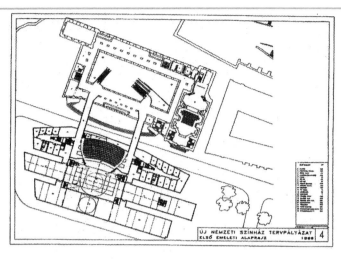

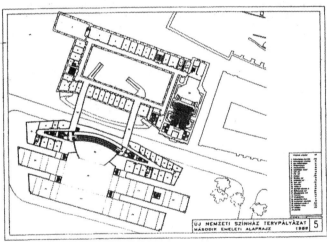

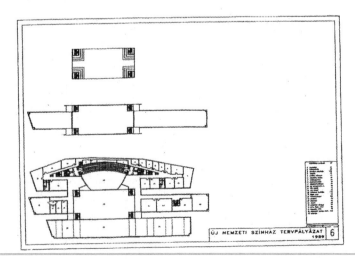

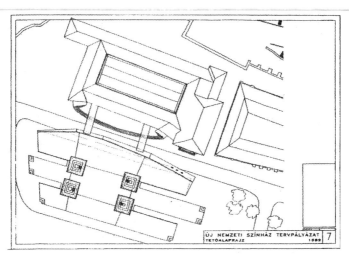

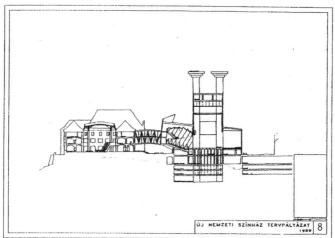

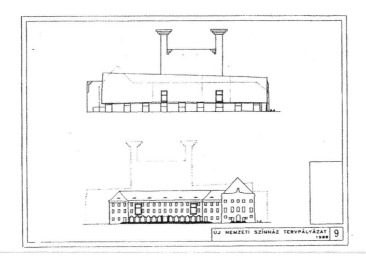

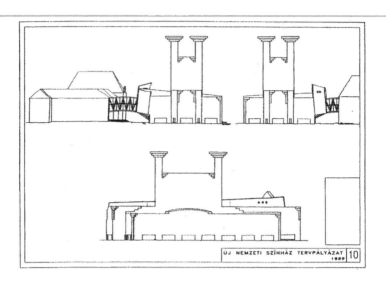

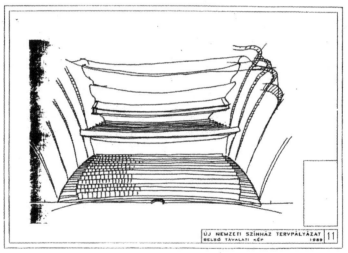

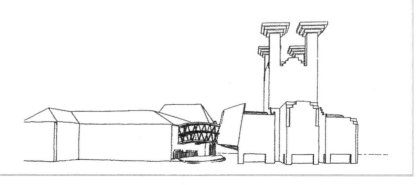

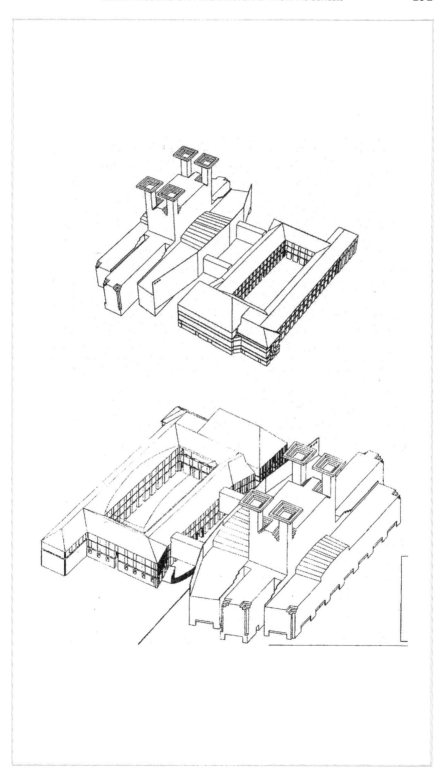

NATIONAL THEATER 3 BUDAPEST

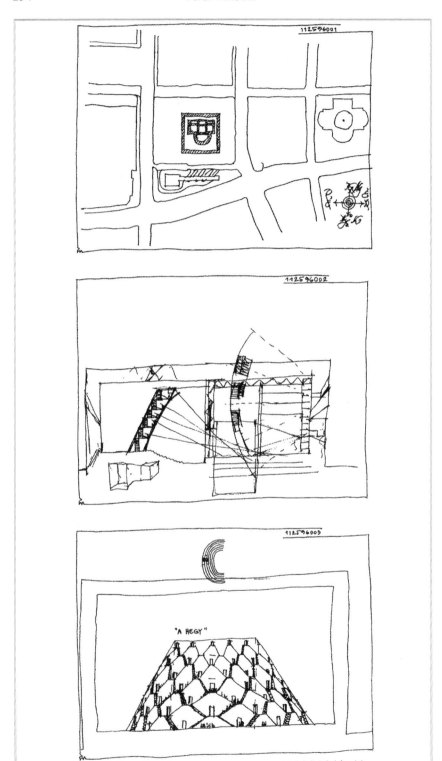

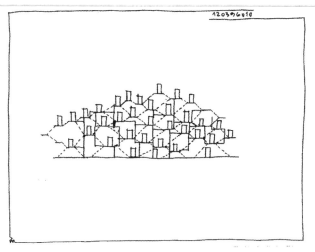

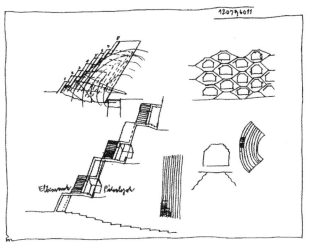

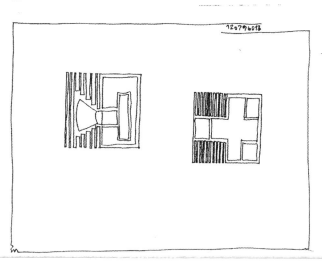

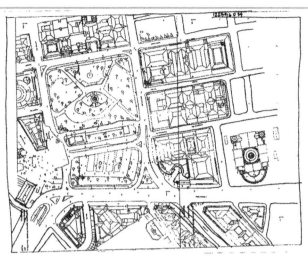

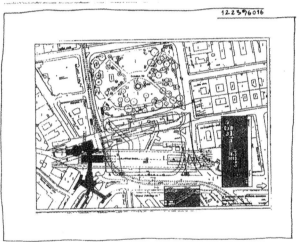

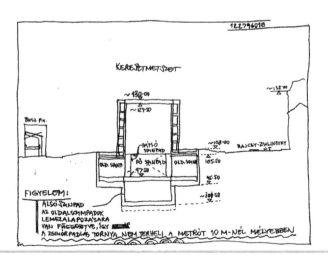

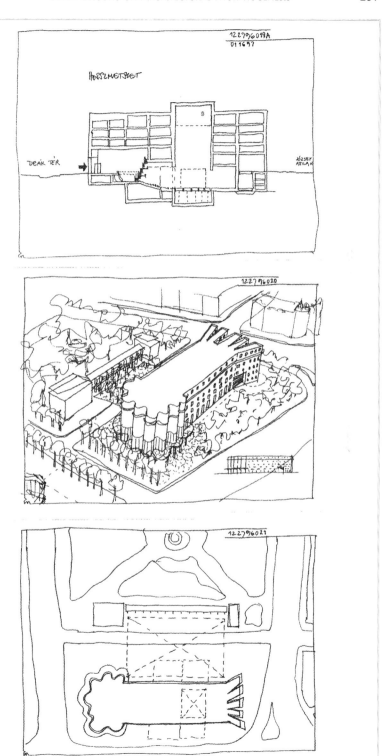

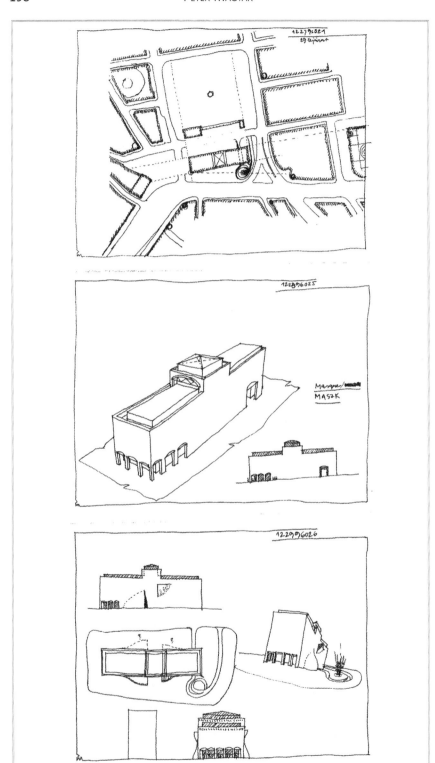

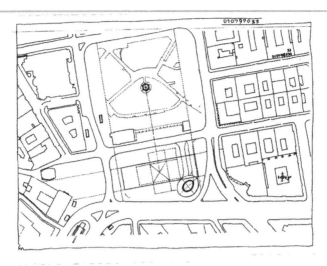

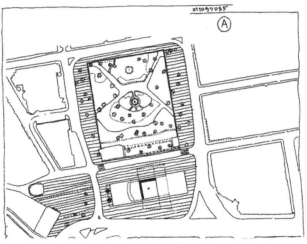

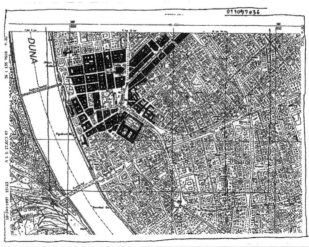

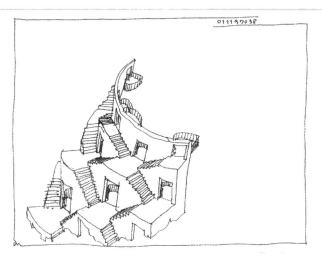

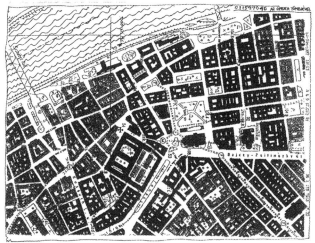

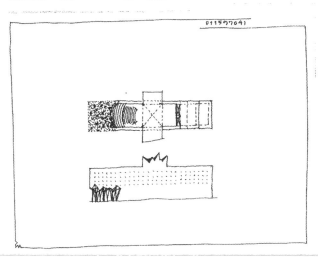

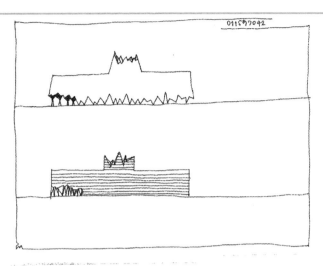

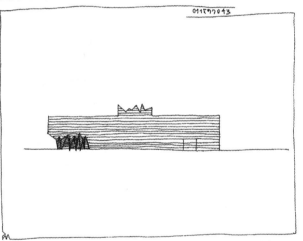

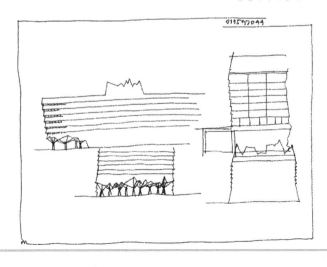

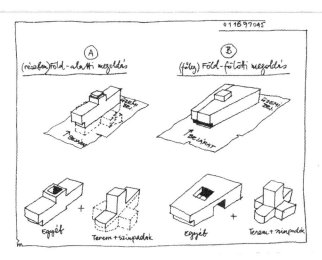

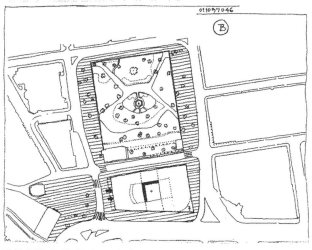

MEGFIGYELÉSEK:
- A SZÍNHÁZ ÉPÜLETÉNEK HELYESBÍTENI ÉS KIEGÉSZÍTENI KELL A KÖRÜLÖTTE LEVŐ ZŰRZAVART;
- TÉRFALAKAT KELL KÉPEZNIE ÚGY, HOGY A KAPOTT TEREK EGYSZERŰ, A GYALOGOS SZÁMÁRA ÉRTELMEZHETŐ ÉS VÉDETT KONFIGURÁCIÓT EREDMÉNYEZZENEK; (AXISOK, UTCA-TENGELY MEGHOSSZABBÍTÁSI A SZÉLES KÖRÚTON ÁT - ÚGY ÉRZEM; NEM EREDMÉNYEZIK A FENTIEKET)
- NEM SZABAD MÉG EGY ÚJABB, ÖNMAGÁRA FIGYELMET FELHÍVNI AKARÓ, "KIABÁLÓ" ÉPÜLETET CSINÁLNUNK;
- MINT A PROGRAM IS ÍRJA, NÖVÉNYZETTEL VAGY MÁS, ESETLEG SZOBRÁSZATI ELEMMEL IS "TUDOMÁSUL VEHETJÜK" VAGY "JELEZHETJÜK" A TENGELYEK BECSATLAKOZÁSI HELYEIT;
- NAGYON ERŐSEN GESZTIKULÁLÓ SZÍNÉSZEKET RIPACS-NAK NEVEZIK - MAGÁTÓL ÉRTETŐDŐ ÉS NEM KIFUNDÁLT GESZTUSOKAT KELL ALKOTNUNK - KÉRLEK BENNETEKET, NÉZZÉTEK MEG JÓL A DEÁK-TÉRI TEMPLOMOT, ÉS TANULJUNK PÉLDÁJÁBÓL;
- A FA'K ÉS AZ ERZSÉBET-TERET KÖRÜLVEVŐ ZÁRT HÁZFALAK NEM KÍNÁLNAK MEGFELELŐ "EGET" EGY OBELISZK VAGY EGY ÚJ EIFFEL-TORONY HÁTTERÉNEK. E MEGOLDÁS KÍVÜL ESIK A TERVEZÉSI TERÜLETEN ÉS AZ ADOTT KÖLTSÉG VETÉS KERETEIN IS.
- A PARK VAGY "KERT" KOMPOZICIONÁLIS ELEMÉT, RÉSZÉT KELL HOGY KÉPEZZE A SZÍNHÁZNAK, DE CSAK NAGYON KEVÉS BEAVATKOZÁS ÁRÁN.
- BELEÉRTVE A MAGAM JAVASLATÁT IS, EDDIG A JAVASLATOK-ÉRDEKESSÉGÜK ELLENÉRE SEM OLDJÁK MEG JÓL A FENTI-ÚGY ÉRZEM FONTOS-KÍVÁNALMAKAT

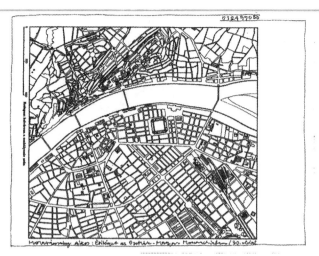

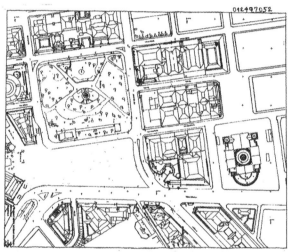

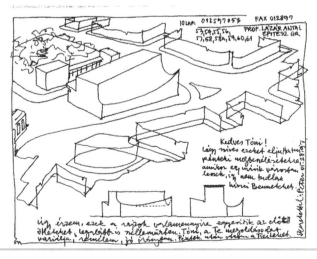

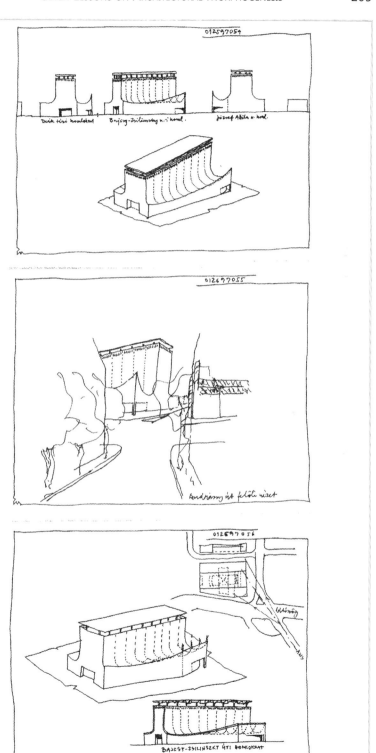

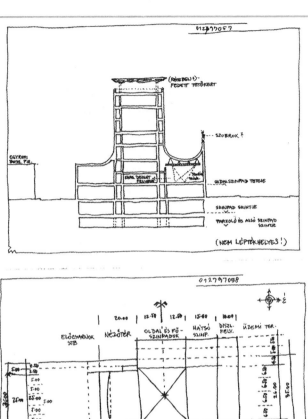

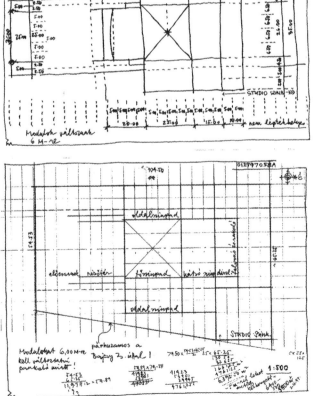

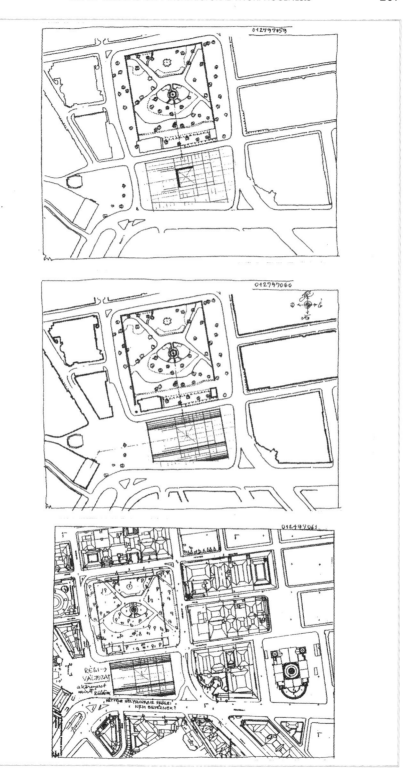

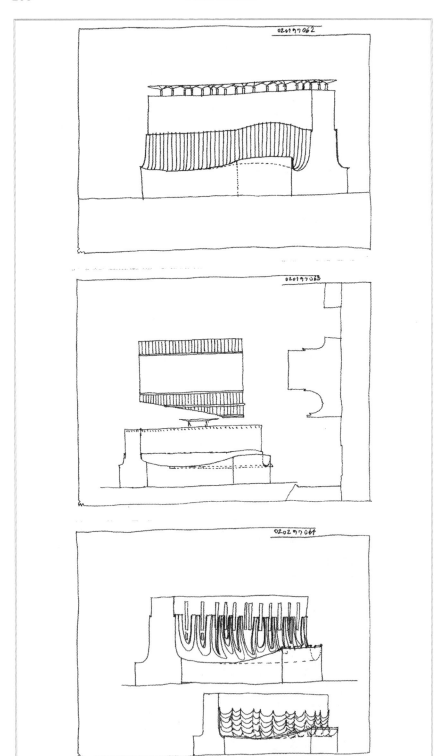

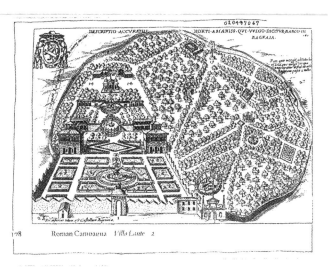

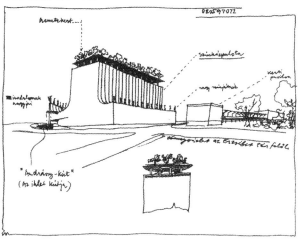

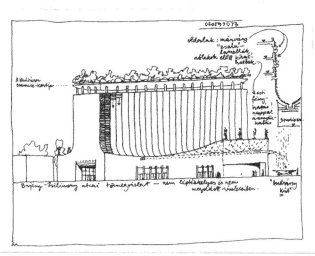

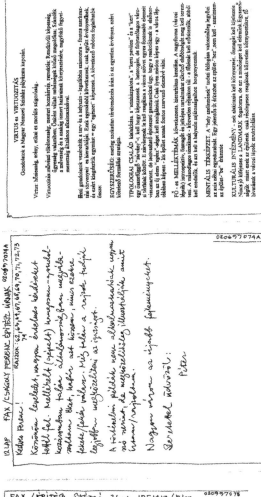

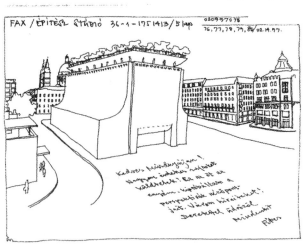

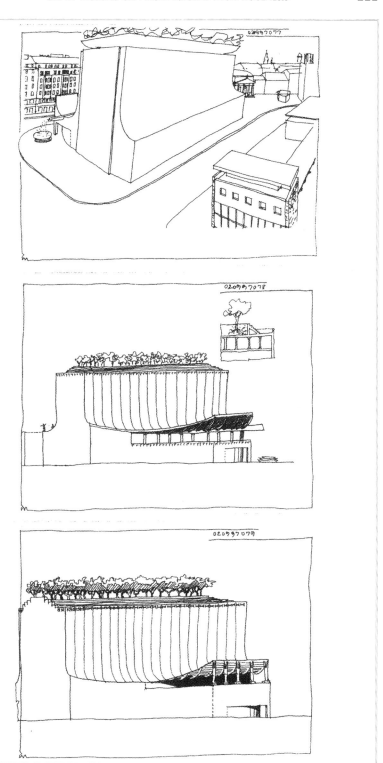

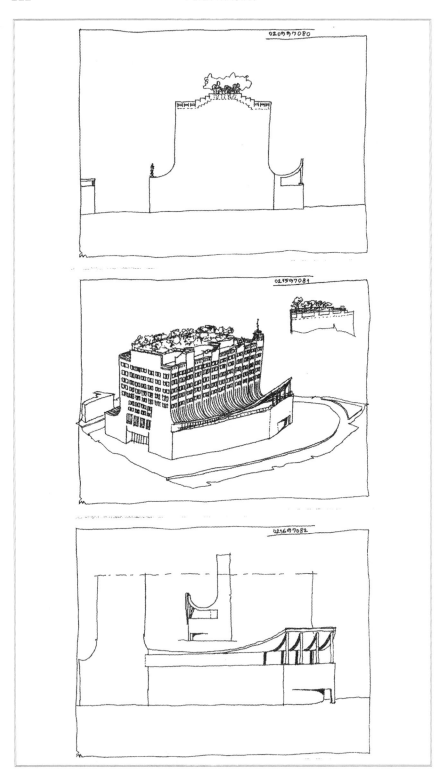

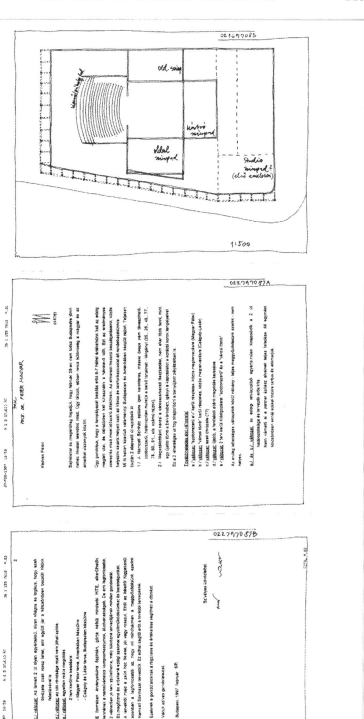

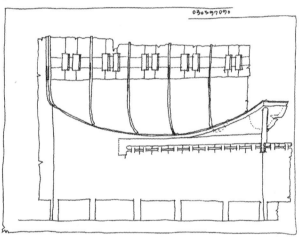

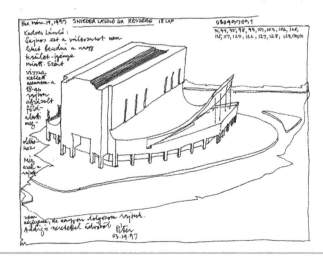

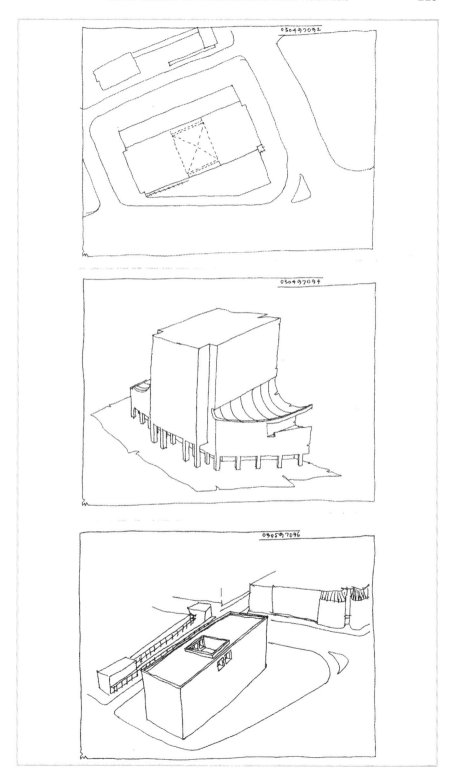

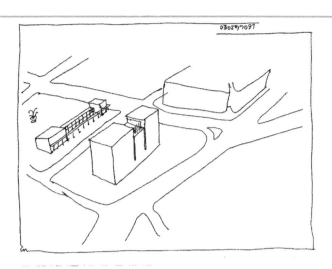

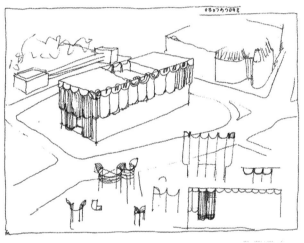

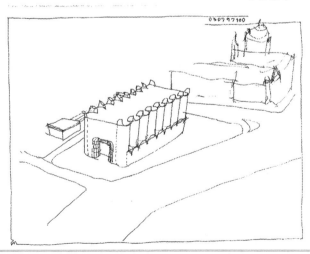

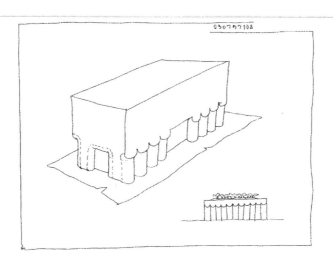

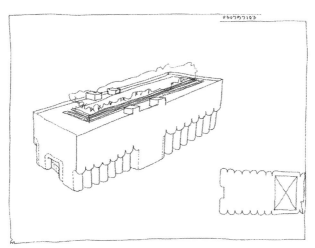

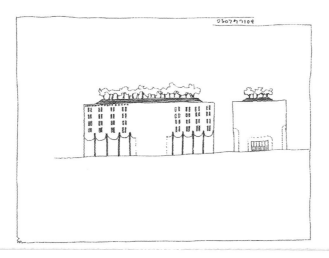

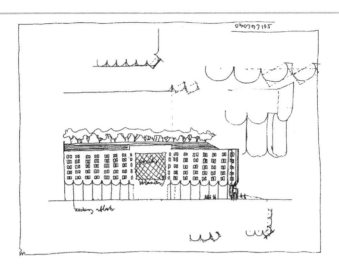

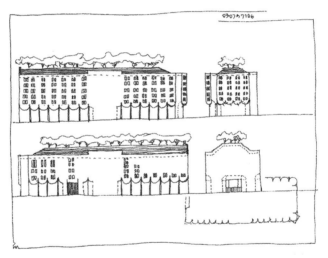

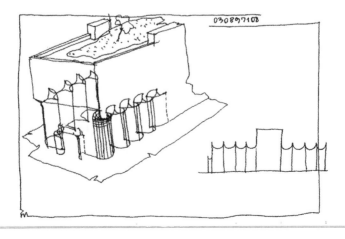

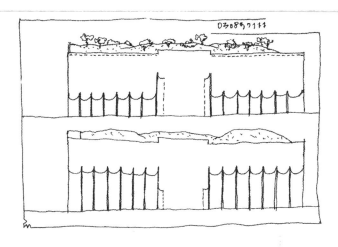

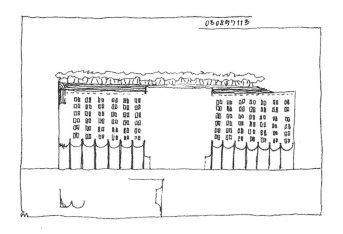

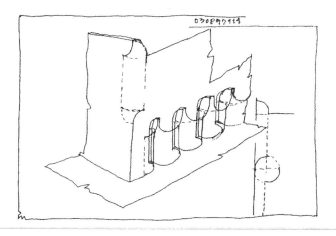

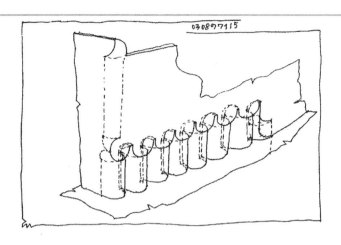

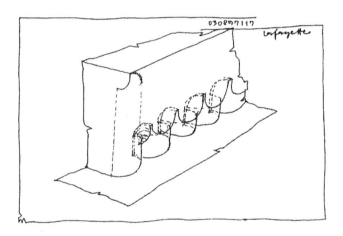

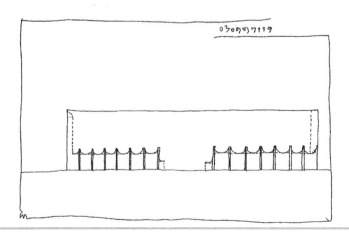

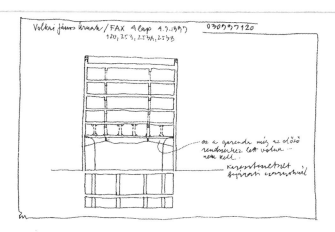

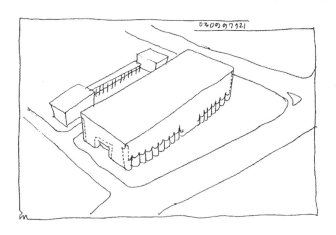

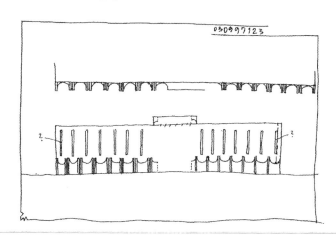

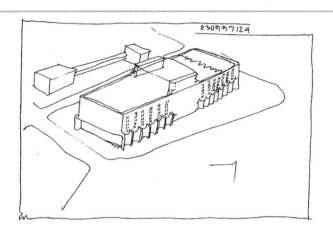

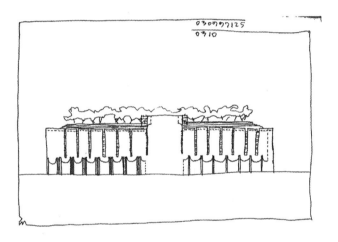

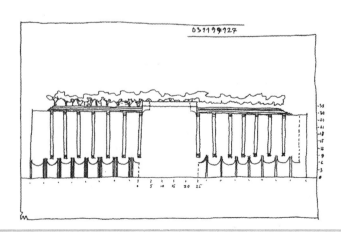

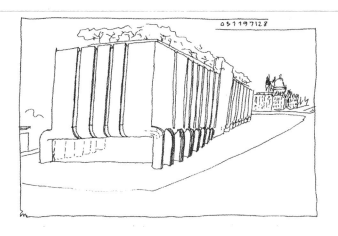

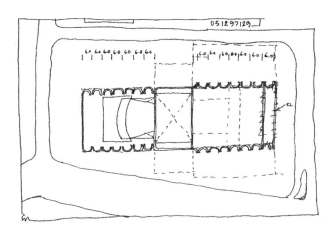

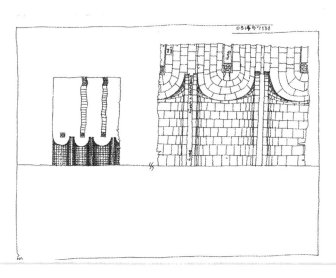

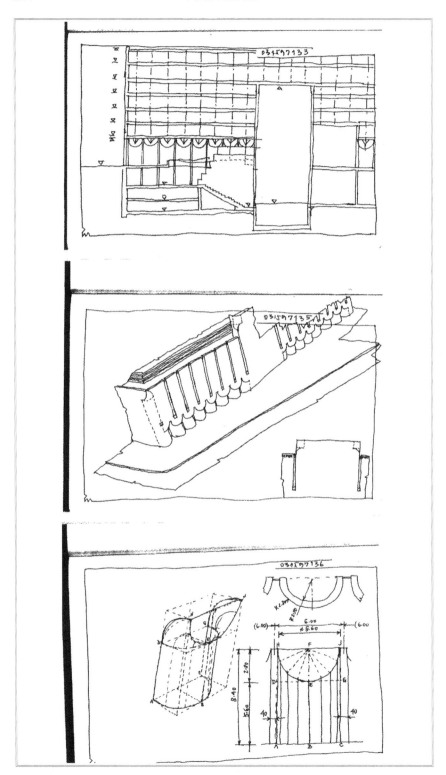

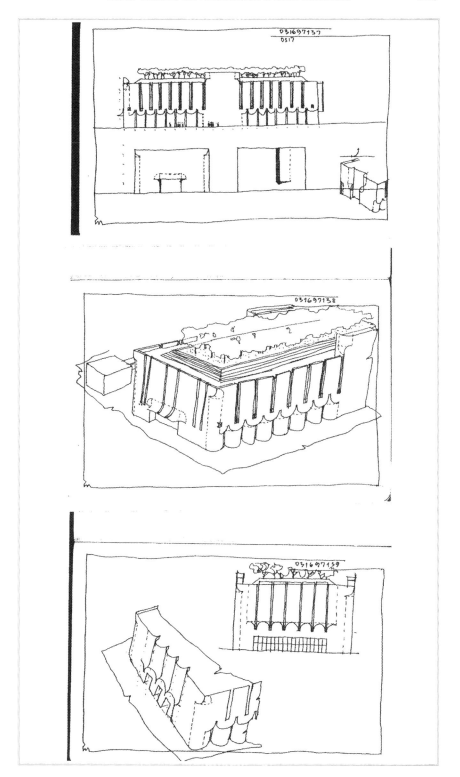

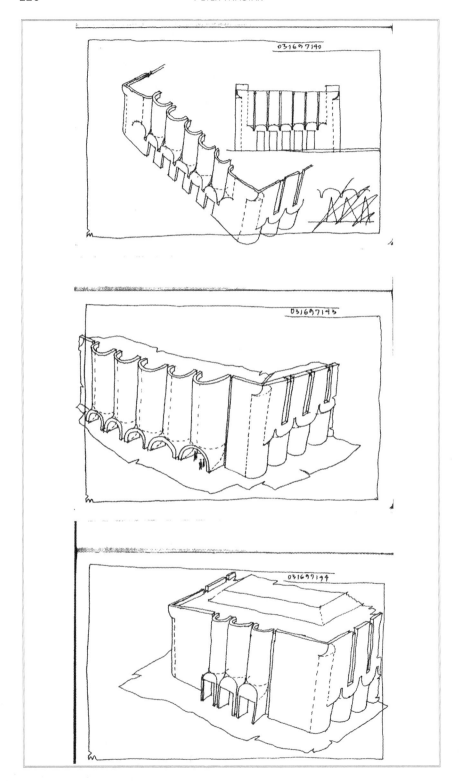

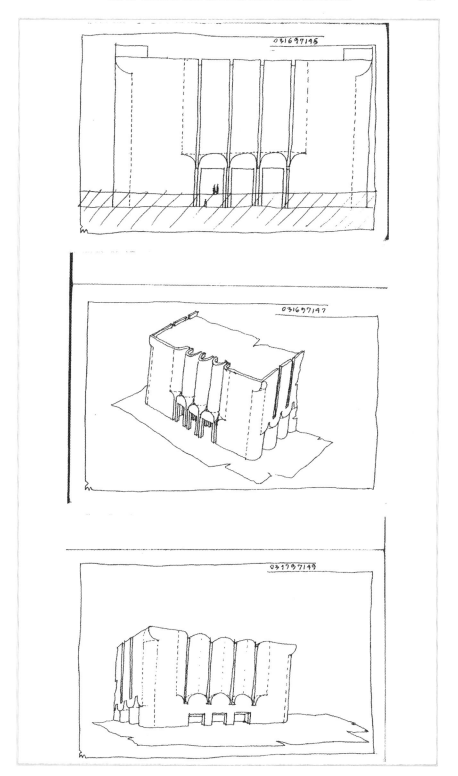

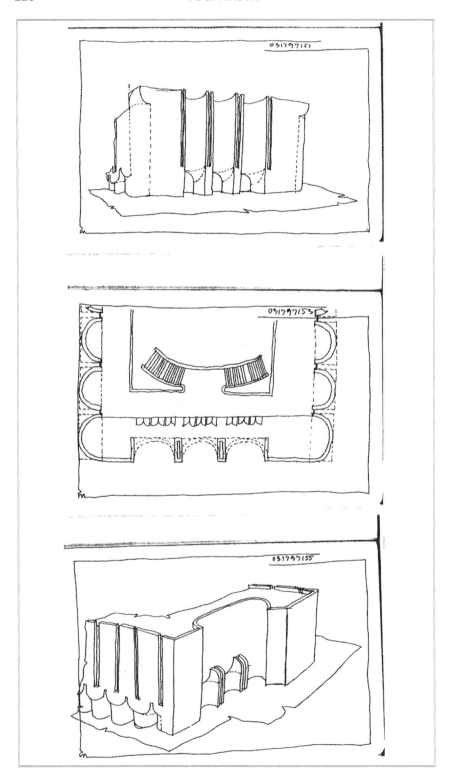

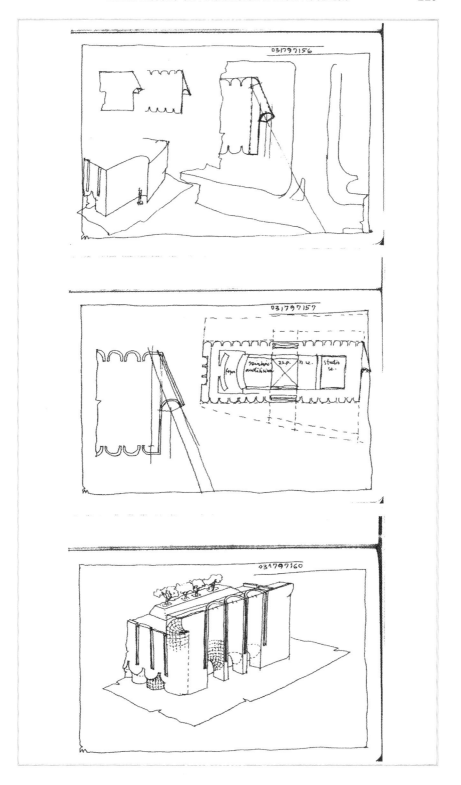

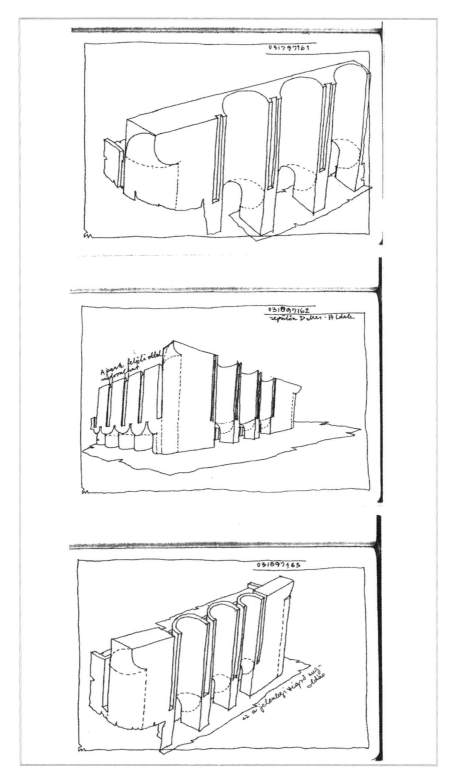

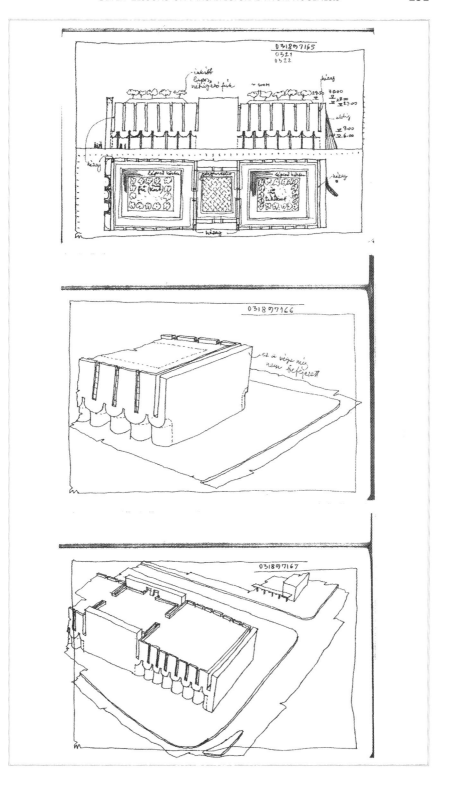

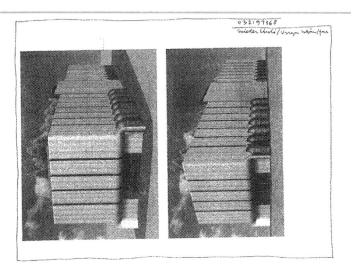

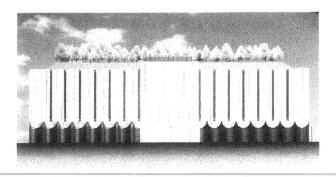

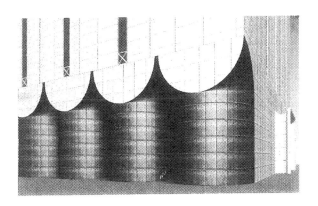

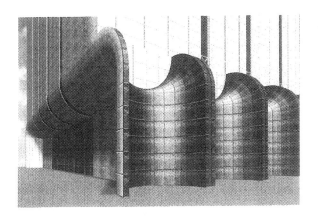

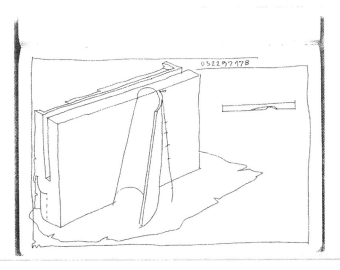

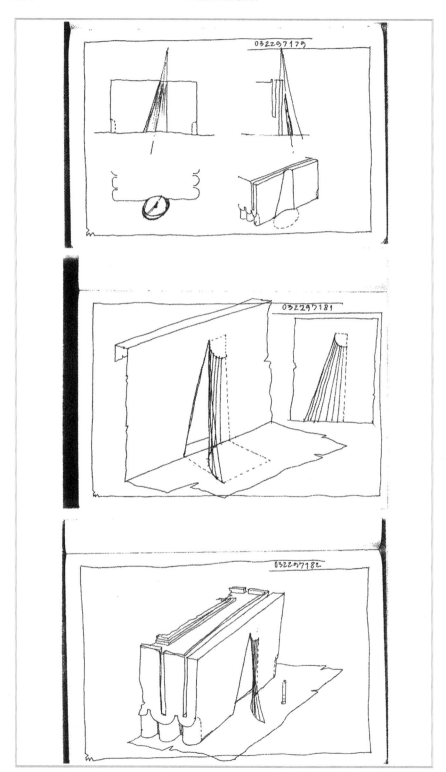

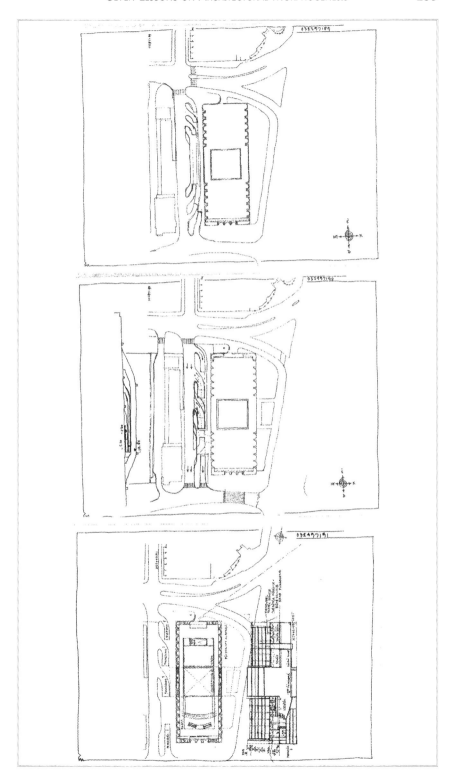

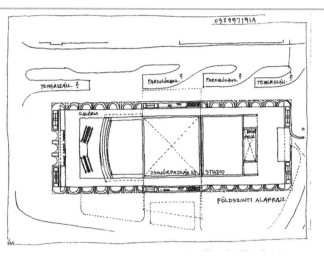

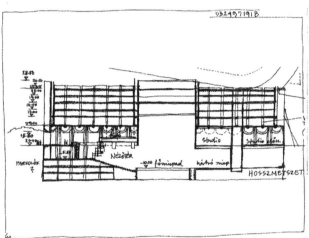

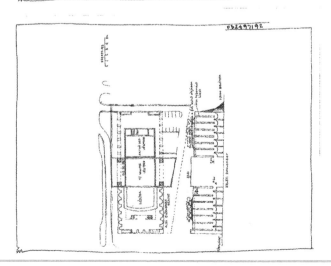

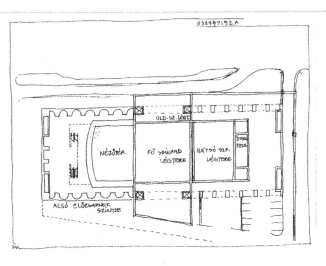

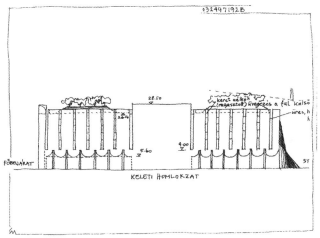

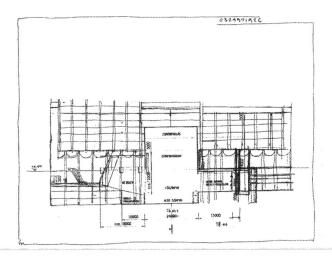

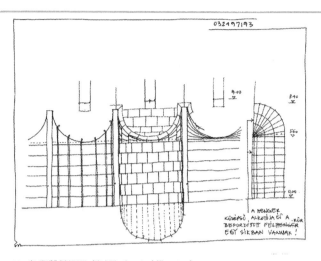

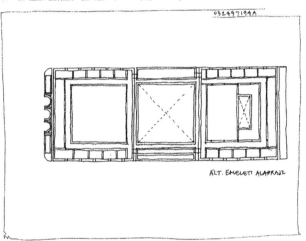

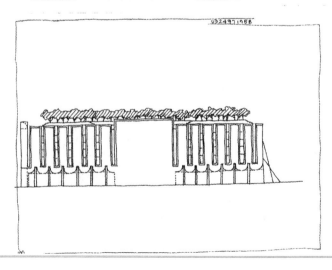

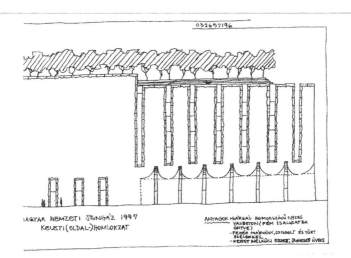

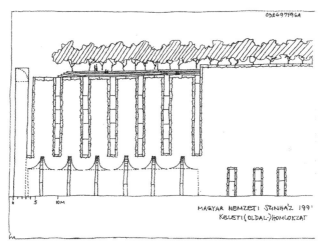

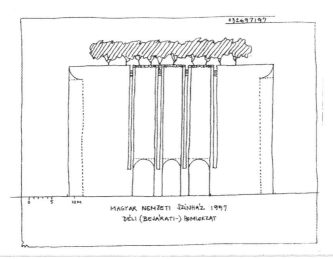

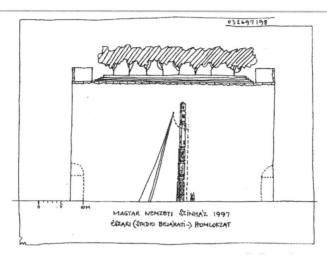

MAGYAR NEMZETI SZINHÁZ 1997
ÉSZAKI (STUDIO BEJÁRATI→) HOMLOKZAT

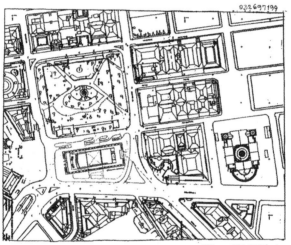

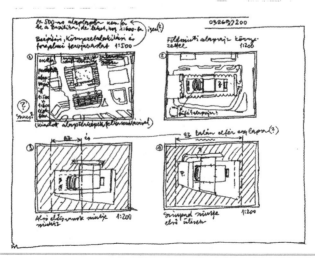

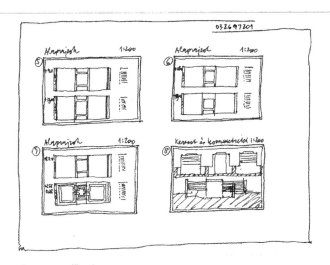

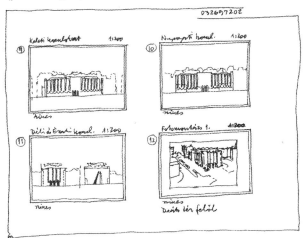

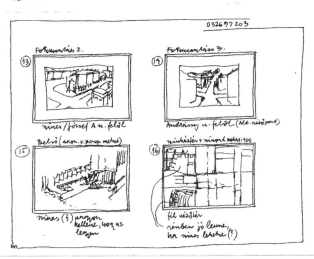

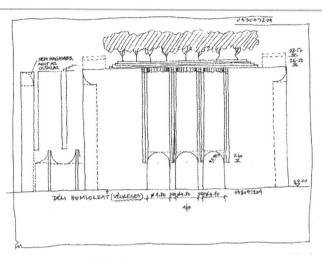

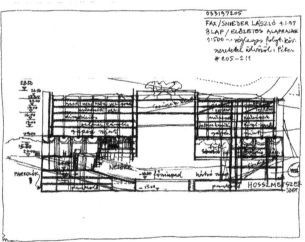

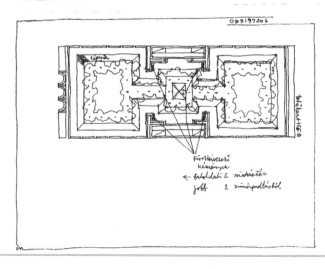

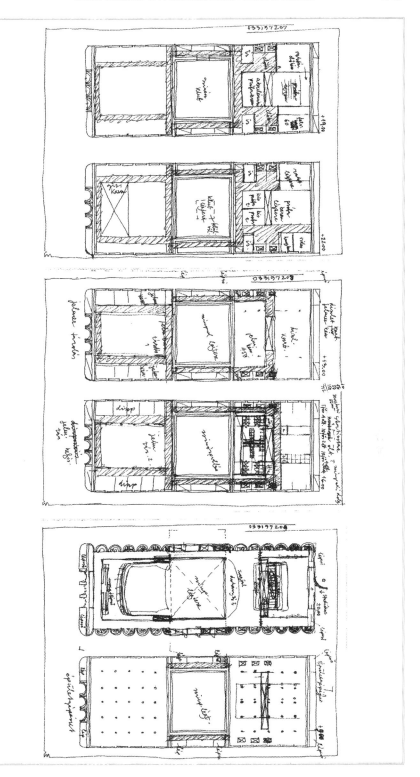

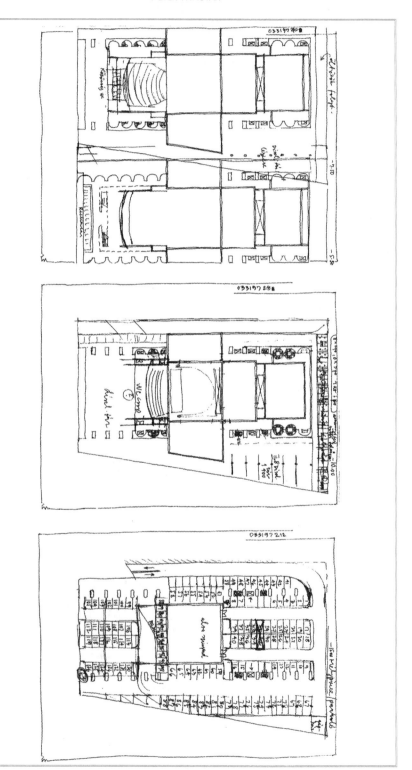

040297214

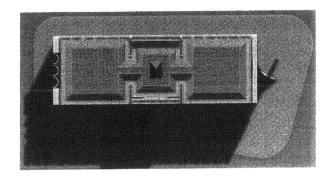

PELHL_1

040297215

HOM_1

040297216

HOM_R.

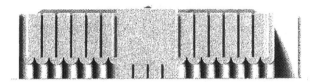

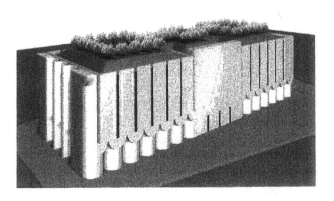

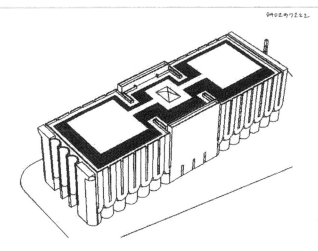

VONAL_1

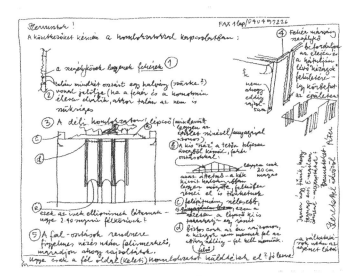

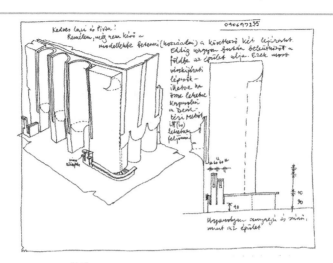

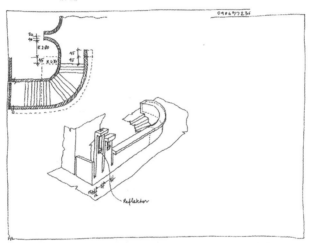

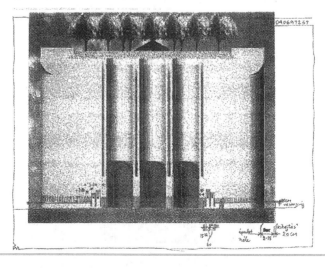

04069723B

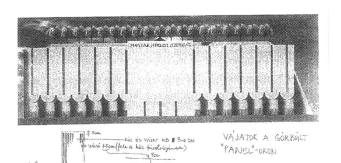

VÁJATOK A GÖRBÜLT
"PANEL"-OKON

0406972 309

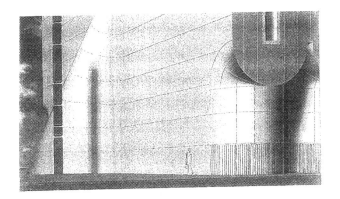

HATSO_1

0406972910

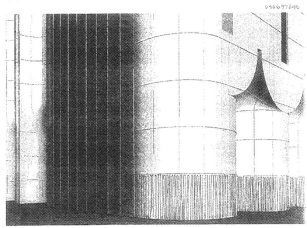

KOZELI 1

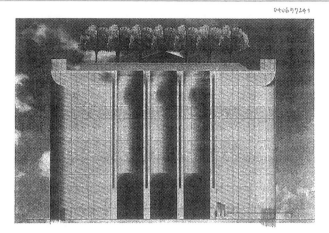

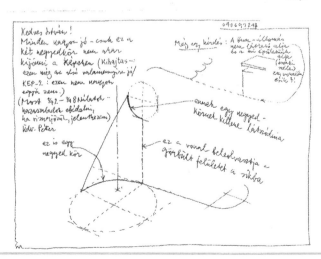

KÉP_11

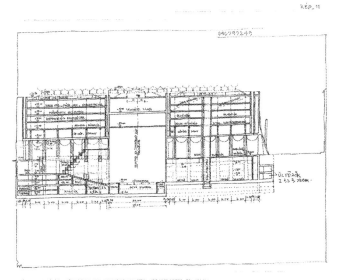

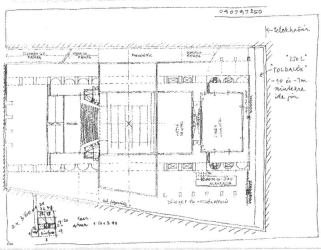

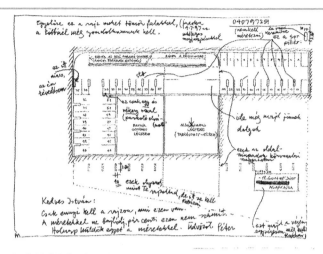

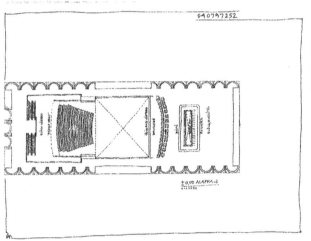

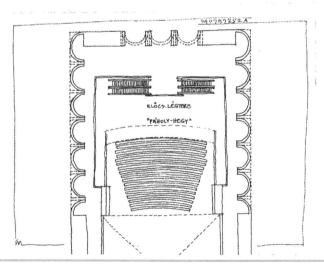

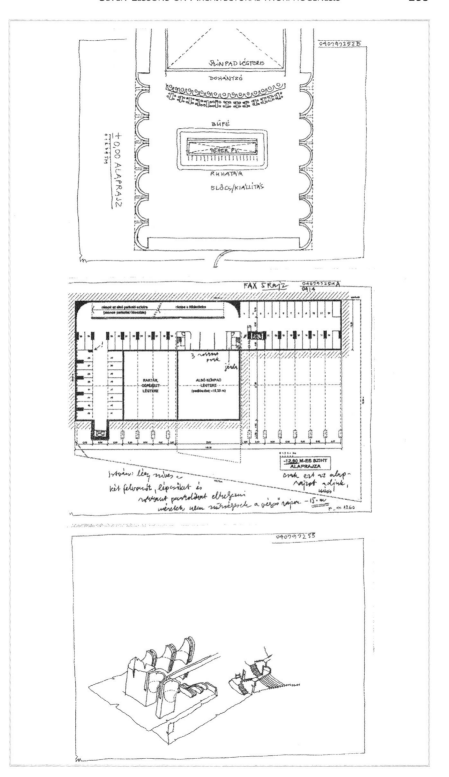

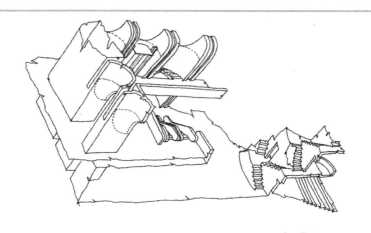

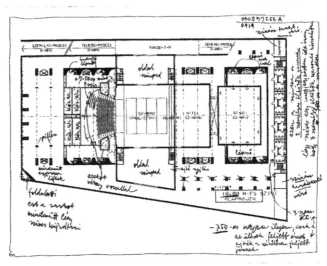

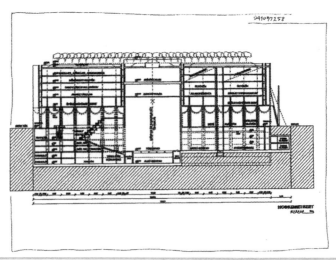

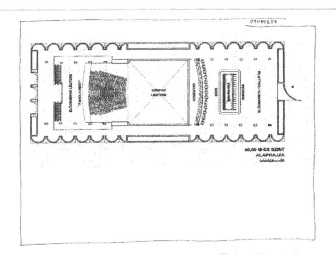

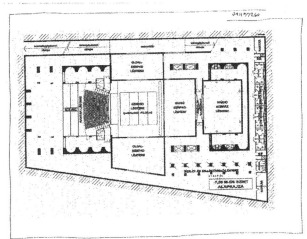

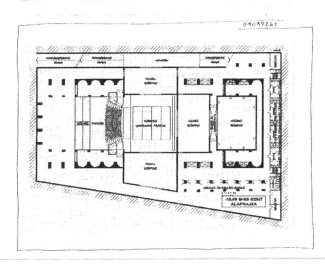

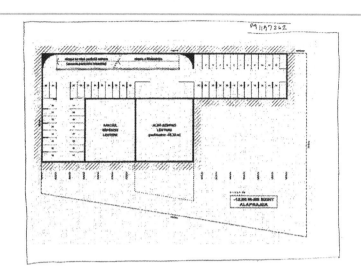

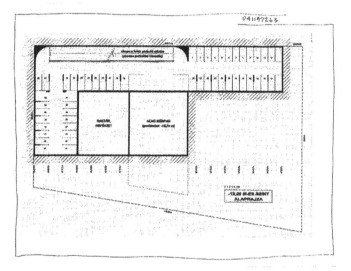

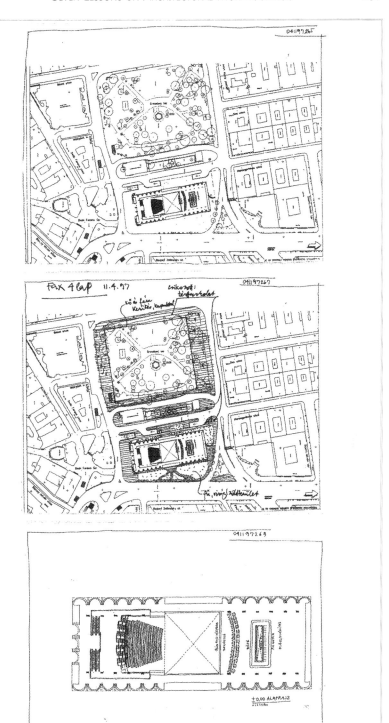

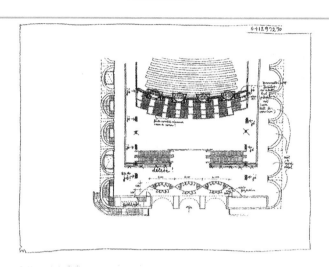

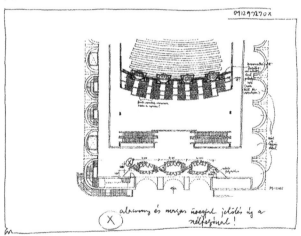

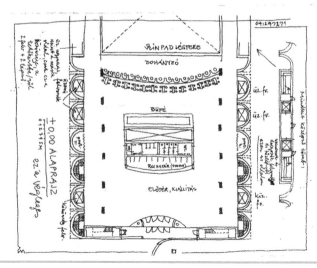

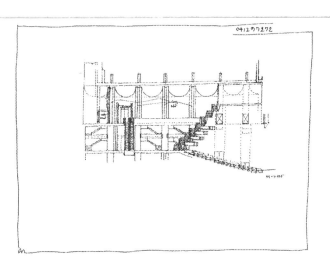

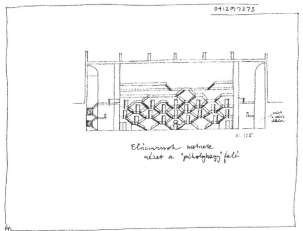

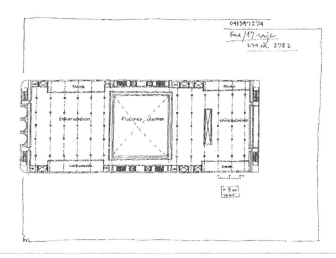

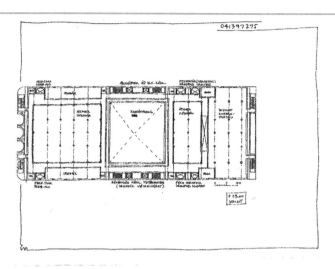

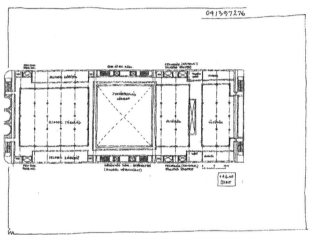

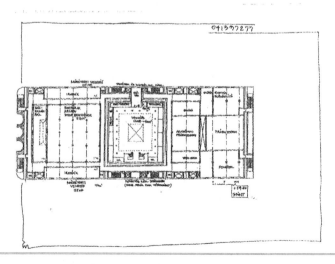

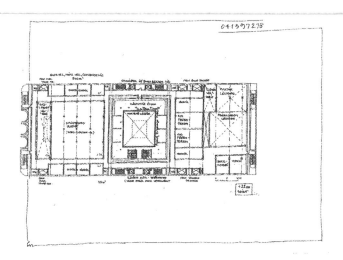

041397279D

SZIN_20

041397280B

BL_15

041397281C

BA_20

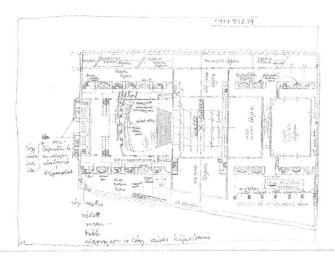

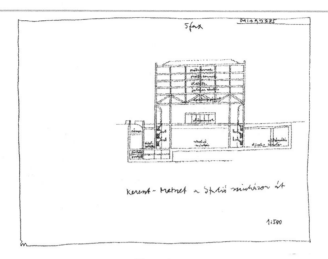

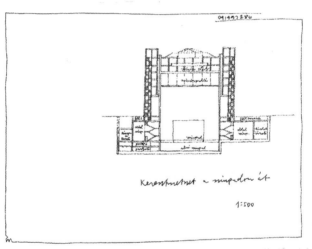

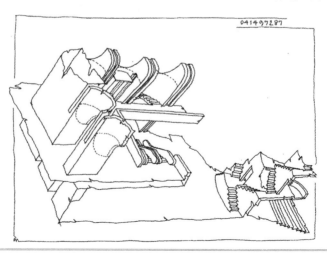

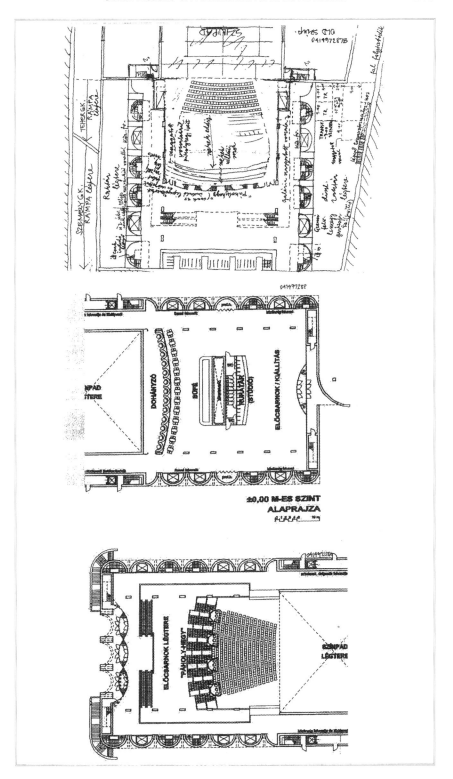

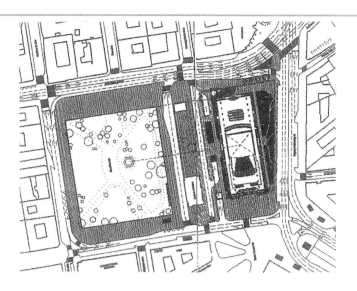

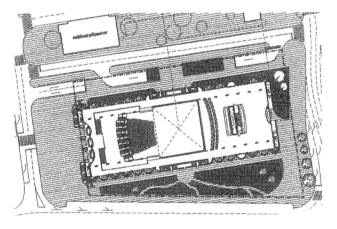

ASPLUND LIBRARY
ADDITION
STOCKHOLM

Recent aerial photo taken before the trees have come into leaf from above the library and Observatory Hill. One view of the proposal should be mounted on this photo.

We Look Forward to Receiving your Submissions!

The Public Library in Stockholm designed by Gunnar Asplund has functioned as the main library in Stockholm since it was inaugurated nearly 70 years ago. The library is a world famous building, breathtakingly beautiful and we view the "20s library" as a timeless concept. There are few public buildings in Stockholm that are so well frequented by people from the entire Stockholm region.

The view of Gunnar Asplund's Public Library increases with every generation of Stockholm inhabitants that uses it. Stockholm is, however, an expanding city and the City Planning Administration estimates that there will be 150 000 more inhabitants by the year 2030. If this is the case, the city will not have a public library that lives up to the ambitions of a sprawling national city of knowledge. On the other hand, it would be disastrous to try to further what the Asplund Library building to power new future demands. In order to be able to maintain and develop the Public Library in the main library of the city and as a natural public meeting place for learning and reading, new activities and functions must be added in a new extension to the Asplund building.

The City of Stockholm hereby invites architects to compete in an open architectural competition in order to be able

to provide the inhabitants of the city with a distinguished public building of high architectural quality. The Asplund Library should form an integral part of a beautifully composed whole. We hope that both international and national architects will be interested and we will, furthermore, pursue this project with the utmost transparency to ensure that the competition also contributes to creating a attractive for a public discussion on how new architecture may enhance the qualities of the expanding city.

We welcome you to participate in the competition and we are much looking forward to the results.

Annika Billström
Annika Billström
Mayor, City of Stockholm

The competition has been commissioned by the Stockholm City Executive Board and is being conducted by the City Planning Committee together with the City Hall Board and Rental Real Estate, the City Culture Committee and the City Development Committee. The competition is being supported in conjunction with the Swedish Association of Architects and will be done in consultation. Rules of the competition will be in accordance with the Swedish Association of Architects procedures.

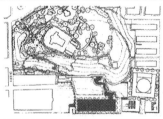

A plan of a final design for the library with the park lying between it and the Stockholm School of Economics. Asplund's solution, structure programmes for the area, rendering e.g., the curiosity box. Schemes, are completed for landscape without disturbance. Four out of the five planned areas buildings would eventually be realised.

Photograph from 2006 showing the contemplative scheme, the park area and reflecting point in front of the library's south facade and the water buildings under one or more facing boundaries.

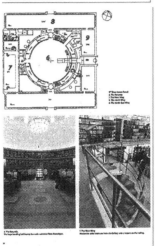

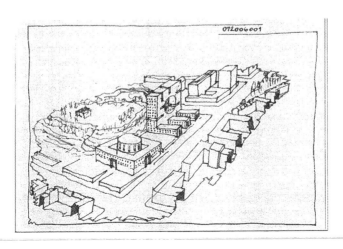

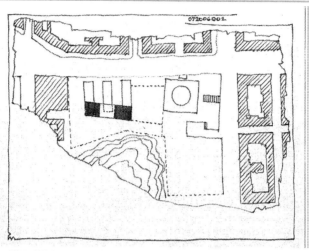

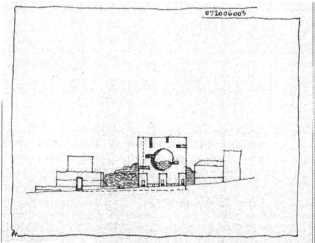

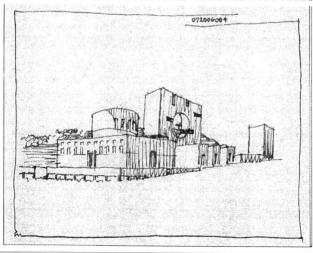

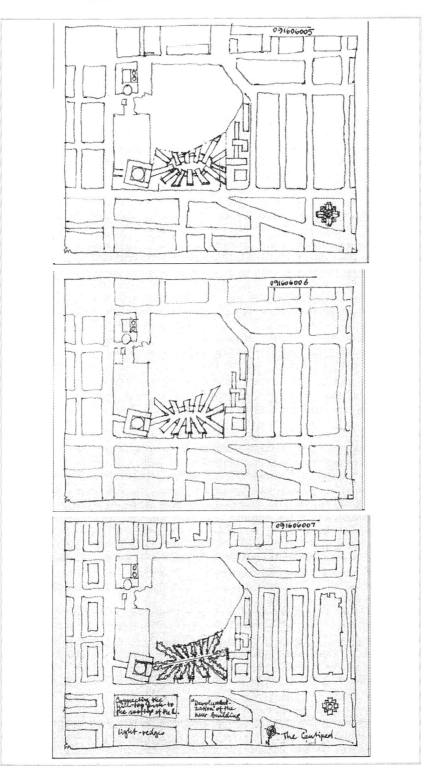

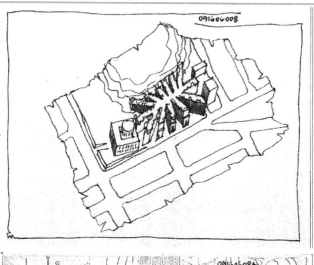

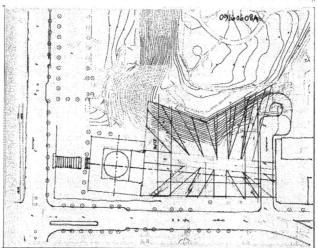

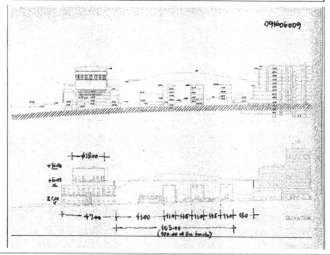

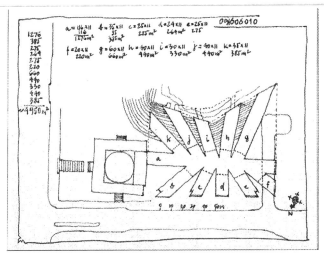

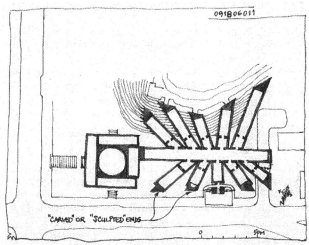

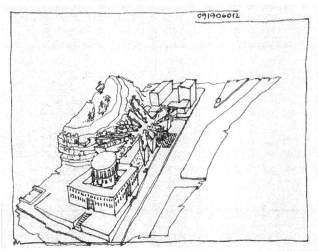

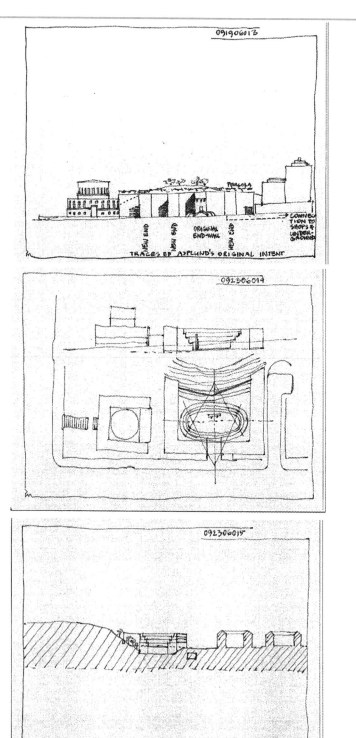

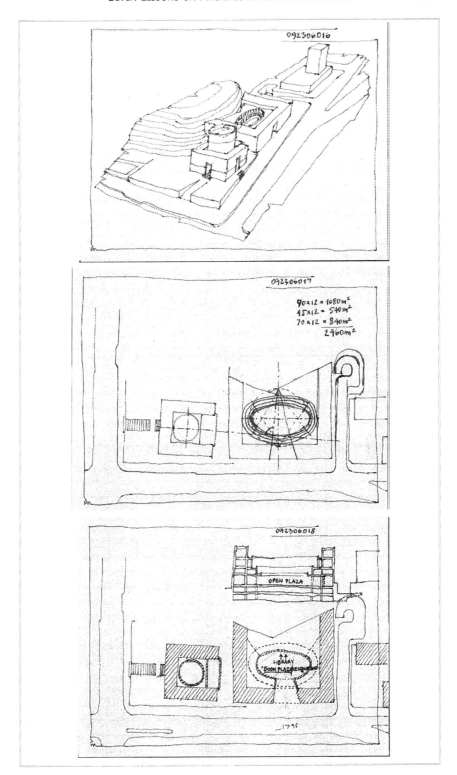

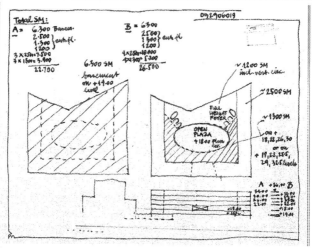

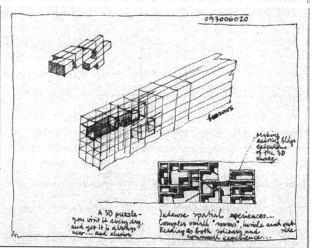

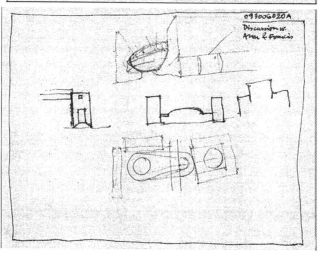

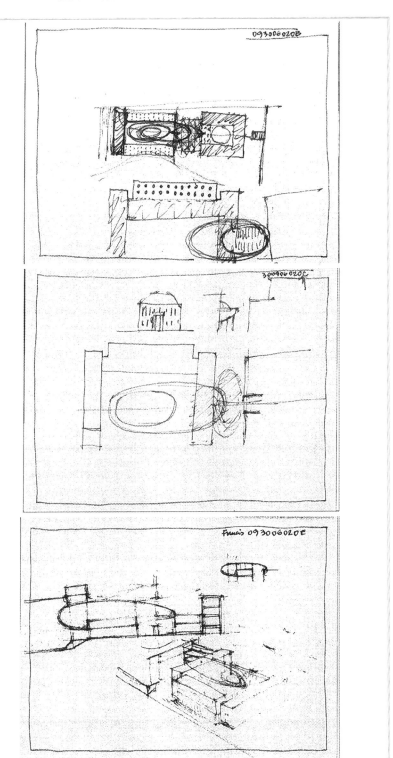

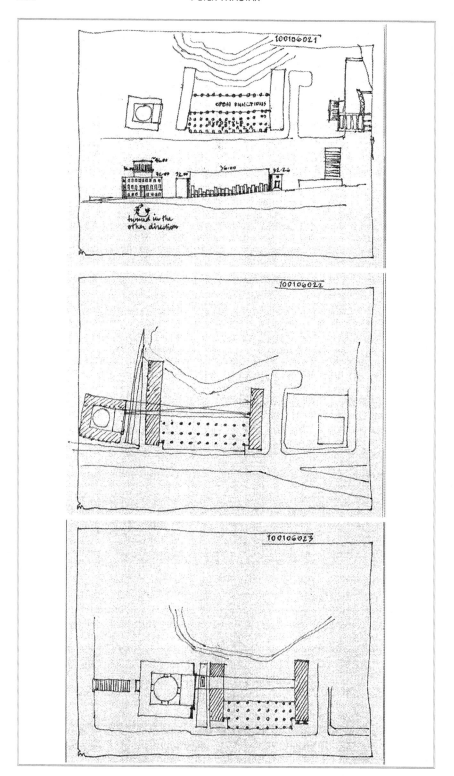

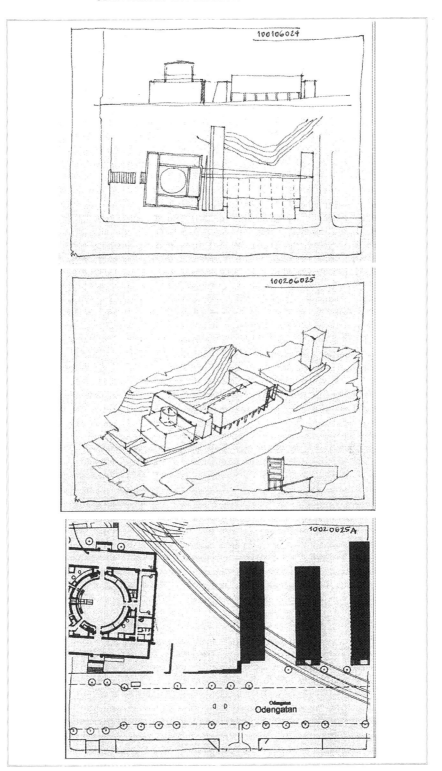

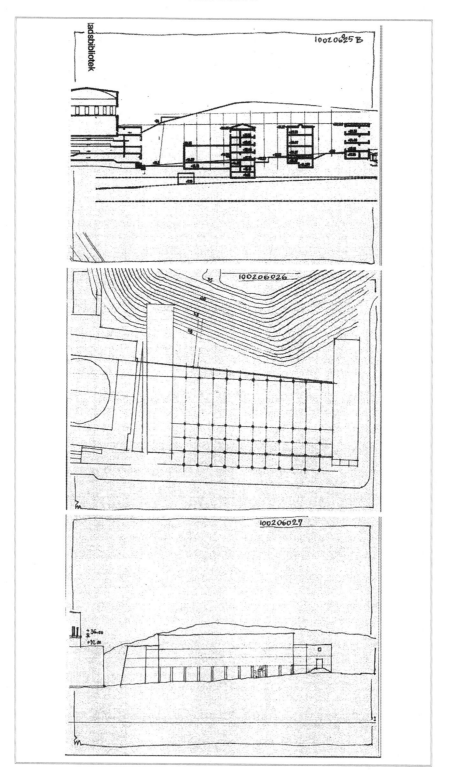

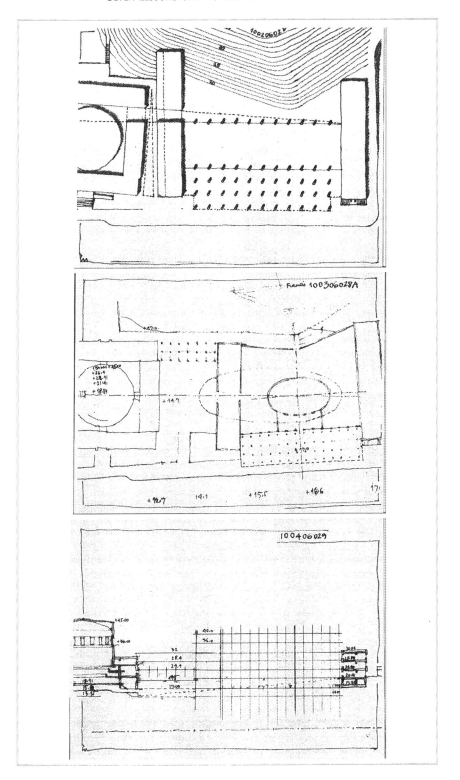

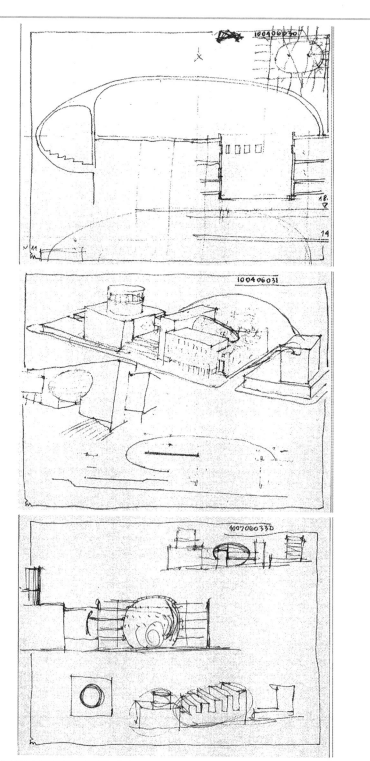

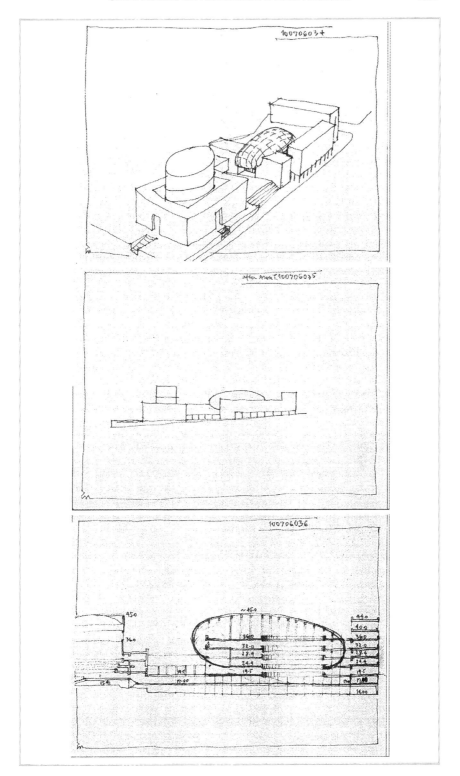

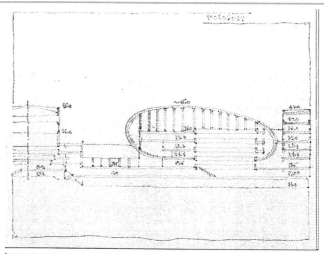

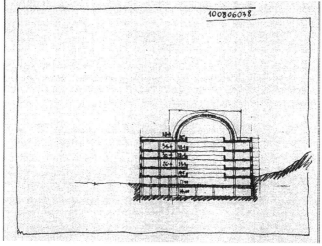

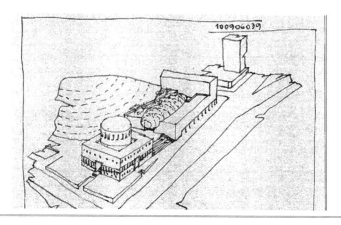

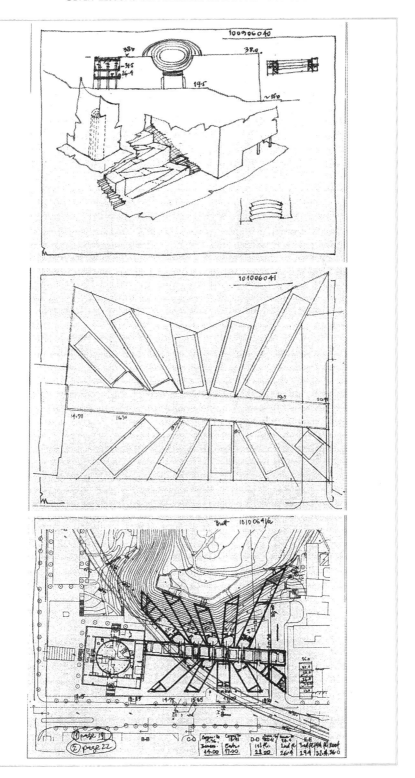

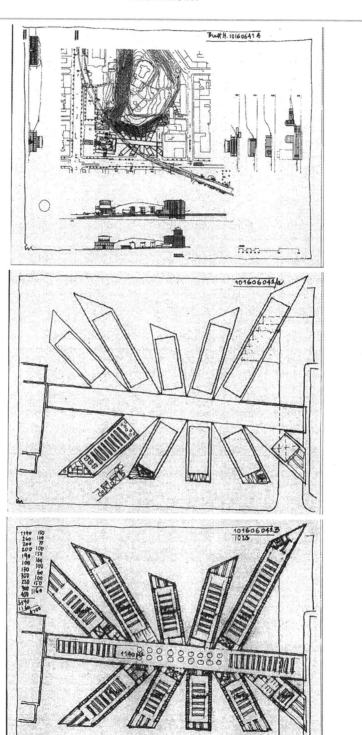

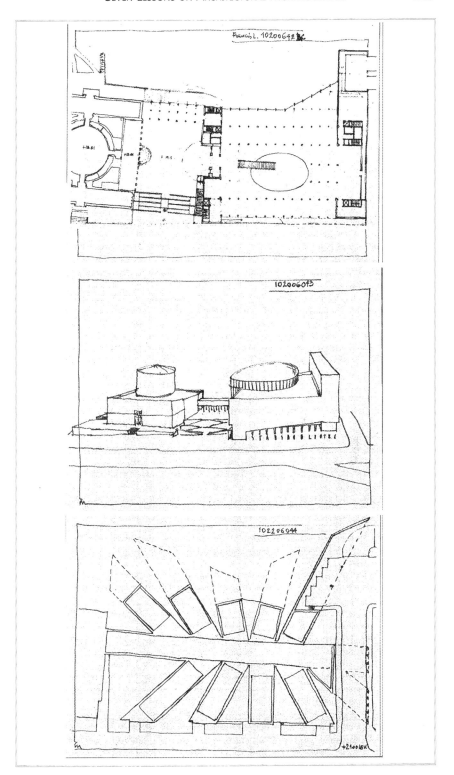

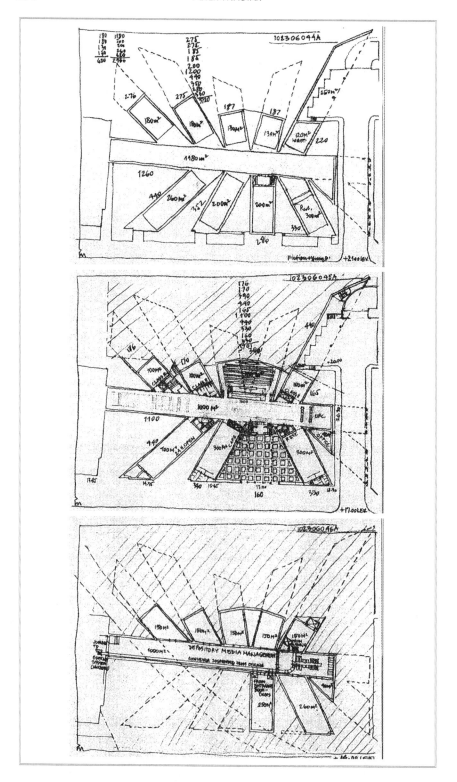

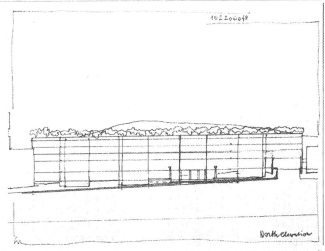

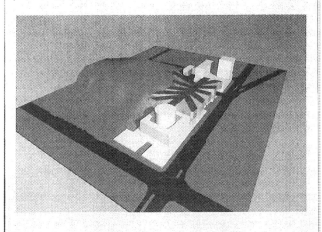

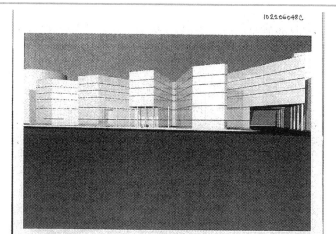

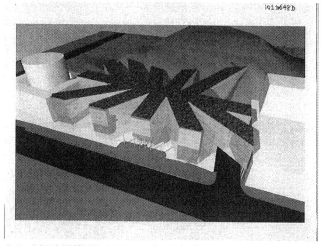

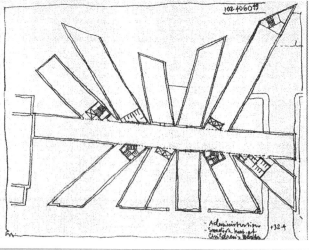

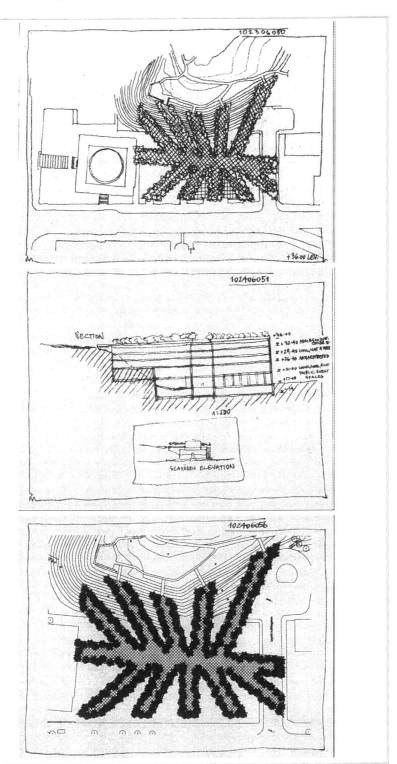

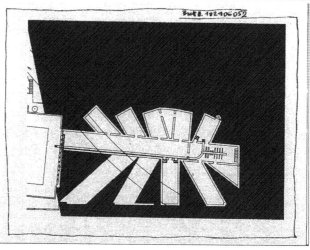

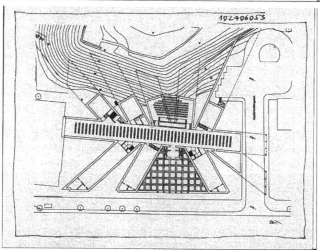

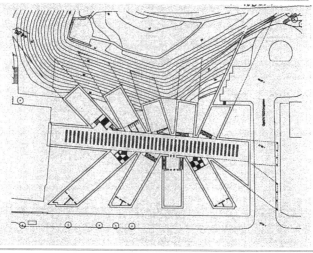

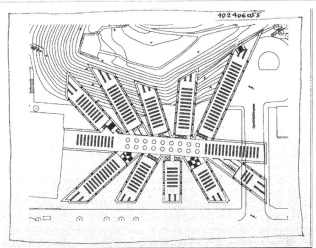

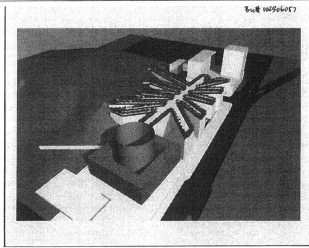

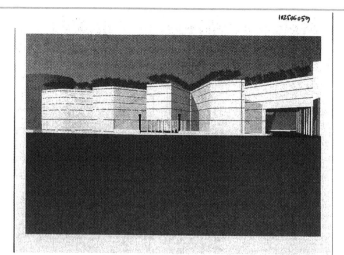

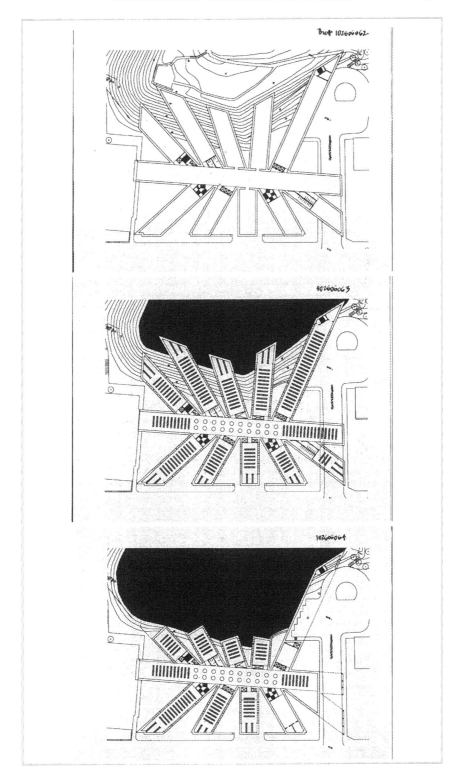

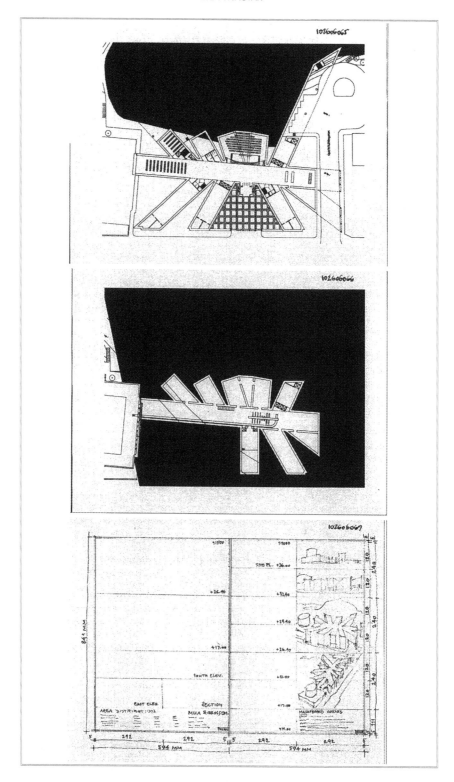

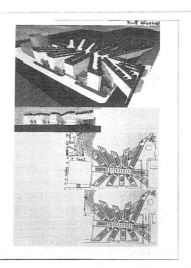

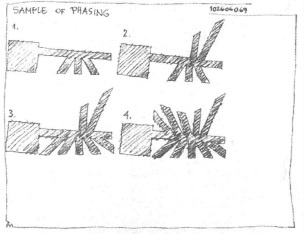

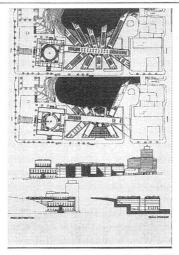

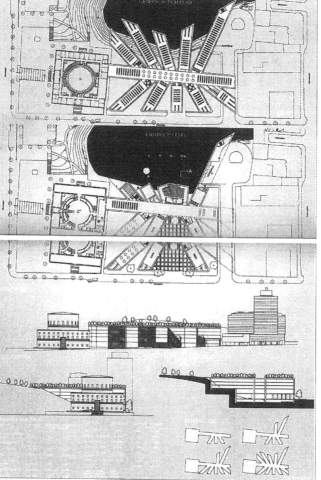

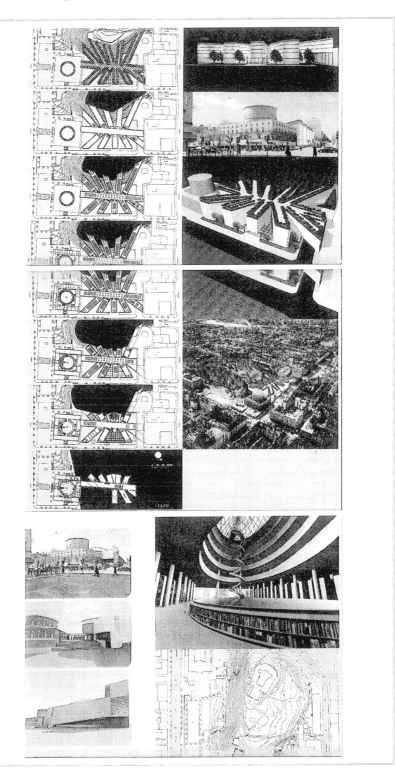

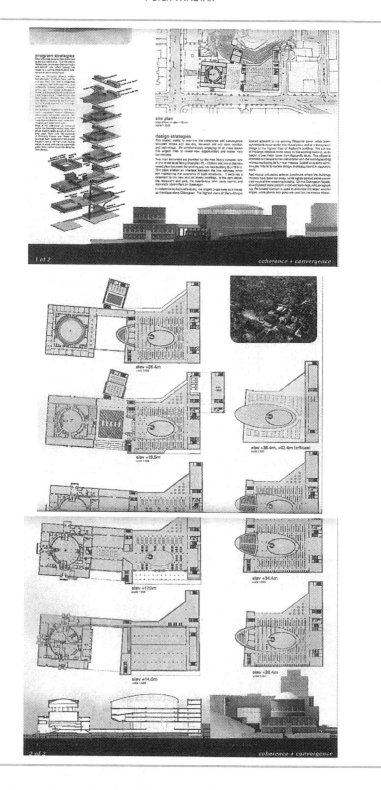

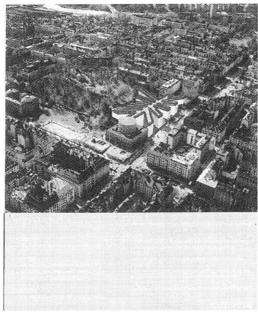

ACKNOWLEDGEMENTS

I express my sincere appreciation for all the persons, who contributed to the projects, included in this book.

The back-cover digital model and photo was made by Mr. Ferenc Kangyal, Architect.

OPERA BASTILLE, PARIS

N. Armington, D. Bogdany, D. Dimitrijevic, T. Flippo, R. Helton, J. Leonard, D. Ray, G. Trout

PUBLIC SAFETY BUILDING, PITTSBURGH

The model and its photo was made by the modeling studio of L & D Astorino Architects

YOKOHAMA INTERNATIONAL PORT

Ihab Elzeyadi, Andrea Novak, Eric Balant, Noreen Murri, Maria Amber, and other members of the vertical studio in Penn State University, whose name wasn't on the drawings.

NATIONAL THEATER 2, BUDAPEST

Architects Gergely Panto and Pier Bandini

NATIONAL THEATER3, BUDAPEST

Architects Ferenc Kangyal, Laszlo Snieder, Janos Volkai and Istvan Varga

ASPLUND LIBRARY ADDITION, STOCKHOLM

Brendt Hoffman and Architect Aron Temkin and Francis Lin. The second version, with the oval galleria, and its computer renderings are made by Aron and Francis

All free-hand drawings are made by author, directly drawn with antique sepia ink on crème colored Crane's paper.